DENNIS RODGERS: A Symptom Called Managua

Nicaragua's capital as microcosm for the country's transformation since the 1970s: shattered by earthquake and the depredations of the Somoza dictatorship, briefly lifted by Sandinista urban reconstruction, remade in the 1990s by narco-traffickers and the returning Miami emigration.

BOOK REVIEWS

TOM MERTES on Jerry Hough, *Changing Party Coalitions*. Ethnic and confessional divisions as the origins of America's political alignments, and the elite strategies that have culminated in today's red–blue polarization.

JOHN FROW on Franco Moretti, ed., *The Novel*. Landmark collection of essays tracing the history and geography of the novel, and relations between morphology, themes and social forms.

ANDERS STEPHANSON on John Lewis Gaddis, *Cold War* and *Surprise, Security and the American Experience*. Diplomatic history as mirror for presidents, with postwar geopolitics recast as morality tale.

CONTRIBUTORS

ALAIN BADIOU: *teaches philosophy at the Ecole Normale Supérieure; books include* Ethics *(2001) and* Logiques des mondes *(2006); see also* NLR *35*

JOHN FROW: *teaches English at the University of Melbourne;* Genre *appeared in 2006*

DENNIS RODGERS: *researcher at the University of Manchester;* Youth Violence in Latin America *is forthcoming in 2008*

ROSSANA ROSSANDA: *founder editor of* Il Manifesto; *books include* Note a margine *(1996) and* La ragazza del secolo scorso *(2005); see also* NLR *18*

ANDERS STEPHANSON: *teaches history at Columbia University; author of* Kennan and the Art of Foreign Policy *(1989) and* Manifest Destiny *(1995)*

ACHIN VANAIK: *teaches political science at Delhi University; author of* The Furies of Indian Communalism *(1997), editor of* Masks of Empire *(2007); see also* NLR *9, 26, 29 and 42*

ZHANG YONGLE: *studying Classical Greek and Roman history at* UCLA

NEW LEFT REVIEW 49

SECOND SERIES

JANUARY FEBRUARY 2008

PROGRAMME NOTES

ZHANG YONGLE: No Forbidden Zone in Reading?

For a decade, the monthly review *Dushu* has published some of China's most incisive debates on the country's culture and economy. Zhang Yongle's survey relates the journal's trajectory to the PRC's dramatic development course and ruptures within its intelligentsia.

ALAIN BADIOU: The Communist Hypothesis

Why does the spectre of May 68 still haunt French discourse? Alain Badiou on the country's *longue durée* sequences of restoration and revolt, and the place of Sarkozy's presidency within them. Lessons in political courage from Plato and Corneille, and a call to reassert the Manifesto's founding wager.

ACHIN VANAIK: New Himalayan Republic

The overthrow of the monarchy in Nepal, brought about by a prolonged people's war and massive popular mobilizations. Achin Vanaik sets out the complex socio-historical backdrop to the Second Democratic Revolution of 2006, the ensuing struggle for a new republic, and the tactical challenges facing the CPN-M.

ROSSANA ROSSANDA: The Comrade from Milan

Memories of war-time resistance work and the political culture of the million-strong PCI in liberated Milan, from one of the founding editors of *Il Manifesto*. Questions and doubts, in this portrait of an unsentimental education.

ZHANG YONGLE

NO FORBIDDEN

ZONE IN READING?

Dushu *and the Chinese Intelligentsia*

T HE PUBLICATION DATE for this long-planned selection of articles from *Dushu*—probably China's leading intellectual journal of the past decade, as well as its most controversial—has turned out to be highly ironic.[1] In July 2007, even as the six-volume *Essentials of Dushu* collection was appearing in the bookshops, its two chief editors, Wang Hui and Huang Ping, were being dismissed from the monthly magazine by its parent company, SDX Publishing. The official grounds for this seemed scarcely plausible: initially there was talk of falling circulation, although in fact the number of *Dushu* subscribers had risen under Wang and Huang, from around 60,000 to well over 100,000. SDX then announced that it was implementing a company policy that required all chief editors to be full-time, rather than complement their work with university teaching, as was the case for Wang and Huang. The company could provide no explanation, however, as to why it had suddenly 'remembered' this policy, which had existed for many years without ever being enforced.

The dismissals provoked a storm of controversy among Chinese intellectuals: debate raged in cyberspace, newspapers and journals over the merits of the 'Wang and Huang era' of *Dushu*. The editors' detractors argued that the two had turned the journal, 'universally recognized' by the Chinese intelligentsia in the 1980s and early 90s, into a platform for a small 'new-left clique', abandoned its elegant prose tradition and rendered it too specialized to be readable. *Dushu*'s supporters, however, argued that Wang and Huang's editorial policy embodied precisely the sort of critical orientation that intellectuals should insist upon in an age of dramatic social transformation, when marketization and uneven development have created widening disparities in the midst of high-speed growth. This selection of the *Essentials of Dushu* allows readers to form their own assessments of the journal's contribution to understanding and evaluating those processes. It offers an overview of *Dushu*'s intellectual preoccupations during the decade from 1996 to 2005, reflecting the major changes brought about under the joint editorship of Wang and Huang. For those outside China, it can also provide a good window on intellectual debates in the PRC during this period: the journal provoked a great many discussions, exchanges and political polemics and, as its title suggests, this selection includes nearly all the essential pieces.

Openings

Dushu—the name literally means 'book reading'—was founded as a monthly journal in 1979, with the famous slogan 'No Forbidden Zone in Reading'. It has published a range of book reviews, memoirs and scholarly essays, running from brief notices—a few hundred characters long—to texts of 12,000 characters (around 7,500 words in English), with a median length of about 4,000 characters or 2,500 words. During the early 1980s, under the editorships of Ni Ziming and Chen Yuan, elegantly written contributions by an older generation of scholars and political essays by open-minded thinkers within the Party made up a significant portion of the journal's articles. *Dushu* was by no means the only platform for intellectual discussion at the time: *Lishi Yanjiu* (Studies in History) and *Zhongguo Shehui Kexue* (Social Sciences in China) were also influential in debating contemporary issues. *Dushu* was known especially for its publication of memoirs and intellectual portraits, which provided a sort of pantheon through which the Chinese intelligentsia could construct a new collective identity.

Despite many disagreements, there was a tacit consensus of outlook among the intelligentsia in this period: they shared a feeling of weariness after the recent revolutionary past and an aspiration for modernization that was summed up in the notion of the 'new enlightenment' as the

---

[1] *Dushu Jing Xuan* [The Essentials of Dushu], *1996–2005*, SDX Publishing Company: Beijing 2007, in six volumes.

character of the age, reflecting an inclination towards liberal universalism; this would be expressed in Tiananmen Square in 1989. The 'new enlightenment' was marked by a certain West-centrism, based on the belief in a linear-historical model of modernization, for which the West's experience was seen as a prime example. Interestingly, many *Dushu* articles in the 1980s tended to look towards Japan: restructured by the United States after 1945, and spared the trauma of political revolution, the Japanese economy had emerged as the second largest in the world. Such admiration was underpinned by an unspoken comparison: in China, revolution had disrupted the modernizing process and caused the country to lag behind. When the Chinese Communist Party distanced itself from its revolutionary past and re-fashioned itself as a 'party of modernization' after 1978, it was therefore seen by many intellectuals as getting back on the right track. For China, the urgent task was to follow the example of the developed countries and integrate herself into the mainstream world order, according to the post-revolutionary consensus. Correspondingly, the glorious mission of Chinese intellectuals was to use the codified criteria of modernity to criticize China's development, past and present.

From around 1985, the introduction of Western concepts and methodologies became a major focus of *Dushu*'s interest: modernization theory, semiology, Russian formalism, Foucauldian analysis, Braudel and the *Annales* school of historiography were a heady brew for a younger generation of intellectuals. The move was part of the wave known as the 'cultural fever' of the 1980s, in which SDX was an active participant; the publishing house produced a famous series of translations edited by Gan Yang, then a graduate student at Beijing University, under the rubric 'Culture: China and the World', which systematically introduced the work of Western thinkers. A similar series, edited by Jin Guantao and Bao Zunxin, was published by Sichuan People's Press under the title 'March to the Future'. *Dushu* ran reviews of many of these translations, including works by Nietzsche, Freud, Heidegger, Sartre and others. At the same time, looking back at the *Dushu* of the late 1980s and early 1990s, one hardly gets any glimpse of the changes that were taking place in Chinese society beyond the intellectual world: the dissolution of the People's Communes, the rise of village and township enterprises, economic marketization, fiscal decentralization and so on; the journal operated more like a salon or club.

Dushu did not suffer as much from the official clampdown after 1989 as some of its sister journals, and continued as a site for 'cultural fever'. The fact that many of the other influential magazines of the 1980s were affected by such pressures and deprived of much of their intellectual vigour led to *Dushu* assuming greater salience. If anything, the commercialization of Chinese society after 1992 probably posed greater challenges to *Dushu*. The readership of most intellectual reviews was shrinking at the time and Shen Changwen, chief editor during 1986–96, turned to a more populist policy, aiming to make its articles easier to read. From 1996, however, when Wang Hui and then Huang Ping were invited to join the journal—initially on a temporary basis—after Shen's retirement, *Dushu* was orientated along more critical and scholarly lines. The pair strengthened the social-science coverage of the journal and encouraged an open engagement with contemporary political and economic issues. They were also more interested in interacting with the international intellectual community than their predecessors had been. It was under Wang and Huang that *Dushu* emerged as a socially critical journal; uncongenial to some, but nevertheless posing questions that indubitably had a wider resonance.

New generation

The two scholars represented a professional as well as a generational break. During the period 1979–96, *Dushu*'s chief editors were publishers and editors, whose intellectual formation was largely in literature, history and philosophy. Wang Hui and Huang Ping emerged from a more formal academic background. Wang, born in 1959, was first known as a Lu Xun specialist, and completed his doctoral studies in the history of Chinese literature. In the late 1980s, he turned to intellectual history. His long paper, 'Contemporary Chinese Thought and the Question of Modernity', originally composed in 1994 but published in 1997, was a shock to Chinese intellectuals at that time and provoked serious debates, due to its critical attitude toward capitalist modernity and its strongly socio-historical approach to the history of ideas.[2] His recent four-volume work, *The Rise of Modern Chinese Thought*, systematically explores the transformation of traditional thinking within modern social contexts. Wang currently teaches at Tsinghua University and is one of

---

[2] Wang Hui, 'Dangdai Zhongguo Sixiang Jingkuang yu Xiandaixing Wenti', in *Tianya* 5, 1997. For an English translation, see Wang Hui, 'Contemporary Chinese Thought and the Question of Modernity', *Social Text* 55, 1998, pp. 9–44.

the best-known scholars in China. Huang Ping was born in 1958 and received his PhD in sociology from the London School of Economics; he now teaches at the Chinese Academy of Social Sciences. He has served as an editor on several international journals, including *Comparative Sociology*, the *British Journal of Sociology* and *Current Sociology*, and has written on social development, modernity and globalization, and—above all—rural development and regional balance in China. Both have a solid background in social theory, which enables them to pose many critical questions about contemporary China. In terms of intellectual formation, they are mutually complementary: Wang is strong in literature and history, Huang in empirical social science.

In part, this represented a wider process of differentiation among Chinese intellectuals during the 1990s. The social sciences became increasingly important in the discussion of public problems from the middle of the decade onwards, and Wang Hui is one of many scholars who moved from literature to social and intellectual history during this period. But *Dushu*'s orientation also reflected the dramatic ideological cleavage that has taken place within the intelligentsia from the mid-90s, when many of its authors began to articulate a critique of China's development path. This was a highly controversial stance, soon dubbed 'new left' or 'post-modernist'. Both labels had strong negative connotations in this context: for a long time after the 1970s, it was almost scandalous for an intellectual to be described as 'left' (as opposed to 'liberal'), because the majority of the intelligentsia had once been the victim of the ultra-leftism of the Chinese Communist Party. Post-modernism seemed even stranger: how could an intellectual criticize the ideal of modernization in a backward society?

Yet the growth of the 1990s produced social outcomes that the intellectuals of the 1980s could scarcely have envisaged. Following Deng Xiaoping's famous 'southern tour' speech in 1992, the CCP threw itself into a reform process characterized by marketization, privatization and integration into the capitalist world order, in which the rapid expansion of export-oriented manufacturing laid the foundation for China's rise to become the 'workshop of the world'; at the same time, the sale of state-owned enterprises, combined with cuts in social welfare to balance the deficit arising from the fiscal decentralization of the 1980s, resulted in millions of state-owned enterprise workers being laid off. As the wave of privatization spread to collectively owned township and village enterprises, millions more peasants lost their jobs and had to travel to the coastal cities to look for work. Disparities grew between rich and poor, urban and rural districts, coastal regions and the hinterland. Pollution worsened dramatically. The high cost of development fell on ordinary people.

It was these conditions that split the relative consensus that had obtained among Chinese intellectuals during the 1980s. The government held fast to the doctrine of 'efficiency first'—*xiaolü youxian*—and forbade any open challenge to this programme. Mainstream economists formed a virtual priesthood around the project of privatizations and social-welfare cuts, and for a long time they almost monopolized the discussion within the intelligentsia and society at large. Any problems emerging from privatization and uneven development were dismissed as temporary hiccups that would be solved by further marketization. For many intellectuals, the rapid growth of the 1990s confirmed their belief in modernization: privatization would lead to economic development, which would in turn give rise to political freedom; this Hayekian–Friedmanite process was understood to be an irresistible tide of world history. Others, however, called attention to the 'dark side' of China's growth model. New voices emerged; the 1980s concept of modernization now seemed increasingly problematic and vulnerable. Disagreements rose to the surface and the shaky intellectual foundations of the old consensus were exposed. As a leading intellectual journal, *Dushu* not only witnessed this transformation but was an important participant in it.

Essentials of Dushu provides a good record of many of these debates and of the strong critical views expressed within them. In contrast to the 1980s, the pages of *Dushu* in its 'Wang and Huang phase' also offer a clear picture of the turbulent developments in Chinese society, as the journal grappled with contemporary problems. *Dushu* has not been the only locus for such discussions: other journals have thrived over the past decade, including *The Twenty-First Century*, *Strategy and Management* and the more left-wing *Tianya*, all of which publish longer articles than *Dushu*. Wang Hui himself has written for all three; his famous essay, 'Contemporary Chinese Thought and the Question of Modernity', which is around 35,000 characters long, appeared in *Tianya*. However, *Tianya* focuses on literature, not social sciences; *Strategy and Management* concentrates on social sciences, not humanities; *The Twenty-First Century* is strong in both, but it is published in Hong Kong and not many people in mainland China have direct access to it. In the early 1990s, *The Twenty-First Century* was the only journal available to those who had fled overseas after 1989 and became a very important resource. It published key debates on conservatism and radicalism in 20th-century Chinese thought, for example, and on China's state capacity. Since the mid-1990s, as journals on the mainland regained their vigour, its significance has declined. *Dushu* for its part has enjoyed an important advantage in being located in Beijing, and has historically maintained close relations with scholars in a wide range of fields. These, however, are not the major reasons for *Dushu*'s significance during this period: the journal's real strength lies in its systematic reflection on the ongoing changes of its times.

Social strategies

The six volumes of *Essentials of Dushu* are organized thematically. The first, 'Reform: Looking Back, Pushing Forwards', focuses on issues of political economy, grouped under four headings: the problems of agriculture, the reform of state-owned enterprises, 'equity and efficiency', and sustainable development—62 articles in all.[3] *Dushu* is to be congratulated for its discussion of agrarian problems, which initiated a national debate. In the 1990s, the government was mainly occupied by reforms in urban areas, and paid scant attention to the problems of the countryside. *Dushu*'s coverage alerted people to the desperate situation of the peasantry (*nongmin*), agriculture (*nongye*) and the rural areas (*nongcun*)—'the three nongs', as they are known in Chinese. Some of the authors see the root of the problem in the dual urban/rural system, under which peasants are institutionally discriminated against; they propose a reform of the system to guarantee equal citizenship, and accelerate urbanization to transfer the agricultural population to the towns—essentially a market-oriented policy. Others express deeper doubts about the market and China's capacity for urbanization. Wen Tiejun, in his 1999 text 'The Problem of the "Three Nongs"', traces the current state of agrarian China back to the contradiction between the country's large population and poor resources, and analyses the major institutional changes in rural areas over the last century. Viewed from this perspective, the official policy of increased urbanization and marketization risks leading to a 'Latin Americanization', characterized by urban poverty, violence and political turmoil. Wen Tiejun thus turns consideration of these problems into a

---

[3] *Dushu Jing Xuan*, vol. 1: *Gaige: Fansi yu Tuijin* ('Reform: Looking Back, Pushing Forwards'), 547 pp, paperback, 978 7 108 026330.

reflection on China's overall path of development. Other authors may not share this outlook, but they too are concerned that the high risk factor of the market may exacerbate the peasants' plight; all are well informed.

Likewise for the state-owned enterprise reforms: many *Dushu* contributors have doubts about a crude privatization policy and point out that it is misleading to attribute the low efficiency of SOEs to public ownership alone, since management practices are also important. Radical privatization has often bred corruption and led to a veritable theft of public property; in these circumstances the introduction of a joint-stock system does not always improve production. A series of articles responds to the 'efficiency first' doctrine, arguing that it has proved a self-destructive force. The question 'should economics discuss morality?' provokes a fierce debate on the nature of economics itself, with both sides urging a re-reading of Adam Smith's *Wealth of Nations* and *Theory of Moral Sentiments*. The role of the economists themselves also comes under close scrutiny: their authority is questioned in the 1996 article 'Theories of Economics and the Art of Dragon-Killing' by He Qinglian, a liberal journalist whose famous book *The Trap of Modernization* discussed the social injustices of China's growth model. Her text provoked a counter-blast from some economists, whose responses have also been included in this volume. This is another debate of which *Dushu* may be justly proud: it was the earliest discussion on this subject in China, and the first time that the intellectual supremacy of the economists was called to account. Even if their views are also represented in this volume, the agenda itself—social inequality, the morality of colossal private enrichment—is a challenge to them.

The second volume, 'Reconstructing Our Image of the World', reflects *Dushu*'s response to the changing international order, both political and economic.[4] The Yugoslav war, the US bombing of the Chinese embassy in Belgrade, China's entry into the WTO, 9-11 and the invasion of Afghanistan and Iraq inevitably led many intellectuals to modify the rosy picture of the Western-led world order they had held since the 1980s. Shu Chi's 'International Terror and International Politics', published in November 2001, analyses the Cold War origins of Islamic fundamentalism, while the Hong Kong poet Huang Canran discusses the intelligentsia's response to the Iraq War and to Western neo-conservatism in his 'Gain

---

[4] *Dushu Jing Xuan*, vol. II, *Chonggou Women de Shijie Tujing* ('Reconstructing Our Image of the World'), 430 pp, paperback, 978 7 108 026354.

the Empire, but Lose Democracy'. The invasion of Iraq provoked a heated debate in China, with some right-wingers declaring their support for the war, while the left denounced it.

Many of the articles in Volume Two—there are 41 in all—grapple with the current path of globalization and explore alternative, more equitable options. Volume Two also reflects *Dushu*'s increasing interaction with intellectuals overseas: there are interventions by Benedict Anderson, Chomsky, Amy Chua, Derrida, J. K. Galbraith, Habermas, Thomas Pogge and Vandana Shiva. There is a very strong debate around the 1997 Asian Financial Crisis. Xu Baoqiang, based in Hong Kong, argues in his 1998 article, 'Re-reading Braudel in the Storm of the Asian Financial Crisis', that the crash has exposed the vulnerability of neo-classical economics, developmental state theory, and 'Confucian capitalism' models; the crisis should be situated within the shifting of world capitalism's 'centre of gravity' eastwards, in the terms of Braudel's structural analysis. In 'From Open Society to the Global Crisis of Capitalism', Luo Yongsheng, also from Hong Kong, draws attention to George Soros's critique of market fundamentalism. Benedict Anderson's 'The Ghost Behind the Miracle' views the crisis from a historical perspective.[5] As the four geographico-political conditions for Southeast Asia's economic miracle—US support, Japanese investment, the PRC's self-isolation and Chinese immigration to Southeast Asia—gradually disappeared, and in the absence of any other effective reform, the miracle finally collapsed.

These analyses were new to most Chinese intellectuals on the mainland, who were still unfamiliar with the notion of capitalist crisis or the debates around deregulated capital flows; 1997 provided much food for thought. Jiao Wenfeng's 2002 article 'The Regulated Market', citing the work of Polanyi and Braudel, argues that the pre-capitalist market economy was deeply embedded in local society and points to the role of the state in breaking down barriers between local markets. The 'regulated market' is the end product of a long social–political process. These discussions were implicit responses to the prevailing Hayekian doctrine of a 'spontaneous order'.

The general aim of this volume is to emphasize that the market is not self-sufficient, it operates in specific political, social and cultural contexts. The

---

[5] Published in English as 'From Miracle to Crash', *London Review of Books*, 16 April 1998.

international economic order is inseparable from international politics. Some texts point out that the ideology of free trade conceals the histori-cal reality that its proponents rose to power through protectionism and colonial plunder. Others propose that the current path of globalization has led not just to increasing disparity between rich and poor but also to the deepening of domestic social or ethnic conflict, as Amy Chua's *The World on Fire* (2004) suggests. The question of global terrorism is viewed in a similar light: a large, oppressed population suffering from uneven development has become the breeding ground for extremism. These discussions generally present a grey picture of the international political–economic order; but the implication is not a return to isola-tionism, but a change in direction on the path of globalization towards greater equality.

Dushu's efforts to restore an Asian dimension to the worldview of Chinese intellectuals are worthy of special note. Asia was a constant presence for Chinese revolutionaries, whether nationalist or communist, during the first half of the 20th century, but it had disappeared by the 1980s; for most intellectuals in the 1990s, the world essentially meant China and the West, with the image of the latter wavering between imperialist exploiters and exemplars of modern civilization. The sole Asian country frequently mentioned was Japan, which featured only as an economic success story. This situation was transformed by Wang and Huang. The 30 *Dushu* articles (around 350 pages) collected in Volume Four under the title 'The Pathology of Asia' cover the intertwining of Chinese and Japanese history, the dilemmas of East Asian historiography, the Korean question, so-called 'Asian values', the political and cultural identity of overseas Chinese, 'subaltern studies' and more.[6] Authors—among them Sanjay Subrahmanyam, Chalmers Johnson, Samir Amin, Arundhati Roy, Partha Chatterjee, Muto Ichiyo, Mizoguchi Yuzo, Koyasu Nobukuni, Kojima Kiyoshi, Baik Young-Seo, Lee Nam Ju, Chen Lijuan, Wang Gengwu and Ma Yiren—come from China, Japan, South Korea, India, Singapore, Malaysia, the US and Egypt; four from Taiwan contribute their reflections on the island's recent history. The wide range of author-ship illustrates the editors' goal: not simply to reconstruct the horizon of 'Asia' for the Chinese intelligentsia but to build *Dushu* as a platform for international discussion on Asian problems—including the ambiguities

---

[6] *Dushu Jing Xuan*, vol. IV, *Yazhou de Bingli* ('The Pathology of Asia'), 350 pp, paper-back, 978 7 108 026378.

and contradictions in the notion of Asia itself. As Wang Hui's account in *Le Monde Diplomatique* suggests:

> The idea is simultaneously colonialist and anti-colonialist, conservative and revolutionary, nationalist and internationalist; it originated in Europe and shaped the self-interpretation of Europe; it is closely related to the matter of the nation-state and overlaps with the vision of empire; it is a geographic category established in geopolitical relations.[7]

The tacit point of reference for 'The Pathology of Asia' is Europe's transition from warring nation-states to economic and political union. While 'Europe' as an identity has acquired some substance, 'Asia' remains a more ambiguous concept. The two editors tend to think that although an 'Asian Union' with political and economic substance is still a distant prospect, it is possible to conceive an intellectual community based upon transnational intellectual networks. *Dushu*'s effort has at least promoted mutual understanding between Chinese, Japanese and Korean thinkers. Many Chinese intellectuals have recognized the importance of the Kyoto School and begun to respond to it, for instance. Korean scholar Wook-yon Lee and Japanese scholar Yaoichi Komori expressed open regret when Wang and Huang were dismissed from *Dushu*. Both spoke highly of the journal's contribution to intellectual dialogue in East Asia during the last decade.

Vision and memory

Dushu's wide-ranging cultural coverage is represented in Volume Three, 'A Compelling Gaze'—there are some 41 articles in all, on theatre, fine arts, architecture, film and music.[8] The title comes from a sharp critique by Zhang Chengzhi, a Chinese Muslim, of the National Geographic Channel's activities in Afghanistan. In 2002, the channel commissioned a programme to look for a green-eyed Afghan girl whose picture had appeared on the cover of *National Geographic* sixteen years earlier, when her country had been the battlefield for a proxy war between the two superpowers. They found her, now a middle-aged woman, and took a series of new pictures. Her gaze, revealing a mixture of fear, grief and

---

[7] Wang Hui, 'An Asia that isn't the East', *Le Monde Diplomatique*, 27 February 2005.
[8] *Dushu Jing Xuan*, vol. III, *Bishi de Yanshen* ('A Compelling Gaze'), 390 pp, paperback, 978 7 108 026361.

suspicion, resisted the interpretative power of the imperialist invaders, Zhang argued—not only the US troops, but also the photographers.

This may stand as an example of the general critical orientation of these texts: the aim is to interpret the 'compelling gaze' veiled by the dominant culture. Although these pieces deal with different arts and forms, there is a shared perspective: images, shapes and rhythms do not simply carry aesthetic values, but may also reveal the social relations of specific historical contexts. *Dushu*'s authors ask: who is speaking, how, and of what; who listens or watches? Their questions illuminate the assumptions, repressions or rebellions that inform works of art. There are discussions of China's new documentary movement, Soviet architecture, Bauhaus design, sculpture during the revolutionary period, Zhang Yimou's movie *Not One Less*, Jia Zhangke's *The World*, contemporary Taiwanese film, music during the Cultural Revolution and in contemporary China.

A good example is Lü Xinyu's 2004 review of *West of the Tracks*, the epic documentary on the decline of heavy industry in Northeast China.[9] Starting from a vivid description of key scenes and an analysis of the narrative art of the documentary, Lü proposes a far-reaching historical analysis of the emergence and decline of Chinese working-class consciousness. Criticizing orthodox Marxism, she emphasizes the importance of the alliance between peasants and workers: in a semi-colonial country like China, peasants made up the major force of the revolution; the first generation of heavy-industrial workers (the 'leading class') also came from peasant backgrounds. Today, both workers and peasants have been tragically marginalized; Lü implies that an alliance between the two will be necessary for the liberation of each. Her theorization is illustrated by an in-depth analysis of the documentary. Not all the writers would concur with Lü's radical perspective; many share the theoretical approaches of their Western peers, including postcolonialism, feminism and Said's critique of orientalism. Nor are these theories all of recent import: *Dushu*'s first encounters with Foucault date back to the mid-80s. But at that point it was still a question of introducing new concepts. 'A Compelling Gaze' shows to what extent these have now been assimilated by the Chinese intelligentsia.

---

[9] A shorter version was published in English under the title 'Ruins of the Future', NLR 31, Jan–Feb 2005.

Pantheon

It is the fifth volume of this collection, 'Not Only for Commemoration', that best preserves a continuity with the old *Dushu*.[10] It carries on the tradition of portraits, memoirs and biographies of scholars and intellectuals for which the journal has long been famous. Among those discussed here are Liang Qichao (1873–1929), one of the leading thinkers of the Hundred Days' Reform of 1898; the educationalist Cai Yuanpei (1868–1940); Chen Duxiu (1879–1942), the founding intellectual of the CCP and editor of *New Youth*; the Confucianist Gu Hongming (1857–1928); the classical Chinese historian Chen Yinque (1890–1969); the Marxist historiographer Jian Bozan (1898–1968); the philosopher Feng Youlan (1895–1990) and the writer Wang Xiaobo (1952–97). There is also a useful discussion of the intellectual community at the Southwestern United University between 1938–46, when the three main universities from the north were evacuated to escape the Japanese invasion.

Interestingly, however, the two major thinkers of the first half of the 20th century, Lu Xun (1881–1936) and Hu Shi (1891–1962), are missing from this volume, despite the fact that *Dushu* published quite a few articles about them during this period. No explanation is given by the volume's editor, Wu Bin. (It should be noted that, while Wang Hui and Huang Ping are the chief editors of *Essentials of Dushu*, there are individual editors for some of the volumes; 'Not Only for Commemoration' was put together by Wu Bin, who became *Dushu*'s chief editor after Wang and Huang's dismissal.) This silence is strange, but not totally incomprehensible. In contemporary China, Lu Xun is the hero of left-wing intellectuals, while the right champions Hu Shi; research on both thinkers has been highly sophisticated. Had both Hu Shi and Lu Xun been included, sensitive readers might have calculated how much weight had been given to each. It is hard to reckon the historical significance of two such complex figures in a single essay without incurring heated intellectual or political disagreement; it may therefore have seemed safer to leave both out of the picture.

Dushu's interest in narrating the life of intellectuals can be dated back to its late 70s origins. At that time, when the experience of the Cultural

---

[10] *Dushu Jing Xuan*, vol. V, *Bujin Weile Jinian* ('Not Only for Commemoration'), 579 pp, paperback, 978 7 108 026309.

Revolution was still fresh, such portraits were often tinted with the memory of political trauma and informed by the longing for autonomous individual space. They were generally written by poets and literary scholars as well as distinguished CCP intellectuals, and composed to a very high standard. *Dushu* was famous for this genre in the 1980s; no other journal published such pieces at a comparable level. The series played an important role in shaping the collective consciousness of the new intelligentsia.

During the decade 1996–2005, the biographical genre remained a significant component of the journal, but not as salient as before. One important reason for this lies in the wider social changes that have taken place since the 1980s. The intelligentsia has risen from being a vulnerable component of the socialist working class to a high position in the hierarchy of post-socialist society; the traumas of the revolutionary period have been left behind. This is the background that needs to be kept in mind when reading this volume, for it does not directly reflect this change of ethos. The articles are still written in elegant prose and in most cases the contributors are highly sympathetic to the thinkers they commemorate: critical assessments are relatively rare. The genre still serves to create an intellectual 'pantheon', a museum of exemplars, through which contemporary identities and commitments may be compared, assessed or affirmed.

Conversations

The final volume, 'To Be Together with *Dushu*', brings together the most important debates that the journal has hosted over the past decade.[11] It covers a wide range of issues: archaeology and Chinese historiography, the contemporary image of rural China, globalization, law, university reform, feminism, the environment, war and terrorism, etc. Some of the texts are transcripts of symposia organized by *Dushu*; others are clusters of articles on the same theme. Volume Six gives a good sense of the extent to which *Dushu* set the agenda for debate in an age of dramatic change. Most topics are fairly specialized, yet they share a common orientation: to deconstruct the codified image of modernity underpinned by West-centrism and linear history; to understand the dynamic of Chinese

---

[11] *Dushu Jing Xuan*, vol. VI, *Dushu Xianchang* ('To Be Together with *Dushu*'), 469 pp, paperback, 978 7 108 026255.

history and contemporary practice; and to explore the possibility of democracy, equality and justice in the current context.

Included here is *Dushu*'s important intervention in the controversies around market-driven reform proposals for Beijing University. A 2003 plan, drafted by an economist, aimed to introduce the principle of competition, encouraging departments to hire overseas rather than domestic scholars, and quantifying the evaluation system to replicate American academic norms. It was vehemently criticized by scholars in the humanities and social sciences. *Dushu*'s symposium on the proposals raised the discussion to a new level. It brought together leading scholars from Beijing and elsewhere to argue the case for the university as an institution for the pursuit of intellectual freedom and innovation, and to question the bias of the economists behind the proposal.

In 2005, *Dushu* organized a further symposium on the crisis of traditional Chinese medicine within the national health system, which brought together famous scholars and physicians in traditional medicine, including Lu Guangxin from the China Academy of Chinese Medical Sciences and Cao Dongyi from the Hebei Academy of Chinese Medical Sciences, and other scientists, among them the chemist Zhu Qingshi from the China University of Sciences and Technology, together with humanities scholars such as the legal theorist, Deng Zhenglai. The discussion covered both policy issues and the different epistemological and methodological foundations of Western and Chinese medicine, defending the latter against claims that it is 'unscientific'. It was also argued that Chinese medicine, far cheaper than its Western equivalents, could expand the coverage of the national health system. Implicitly at stake here is China's tumultuous recent history. During the Cultural Revolution, Mao Zedong encouraged traditional medicine and used it to build up a relatively successful healthcare system. After the past two decades of market reform, however, medical care has become too expensive for ordinary people to afford. Although the speakers did not make such an explicit comparison, readers were left to consider the implications of the debate and to evaluate for themselves the importance of China's socialist legacy. *Dushu*'s role was once again to bring together high levels of professional knowledge and critical intellectual reflection to inform the public discussion. Again, 'To Be Together with *Dushu*' includes a selection of international interlocutors, including Habermas, Derrida, Perry Anderson, Mark Selden, Michael Hardt and Antonio Negri.

Not all the overseas authors who appeared in *Dushu* during Wang and Huang's editorship are included in these six volumes. Alasdair MacIntyre and Immanuel Wallerstein are two contributors who are not represented here. The reason may be that the selected topics leave no margin for debates on virtue and community, or on the history of the social sciences; perhaps the editors judged that *Dushu*'s treatment of these questions was not mature enough for inclusion. However, some important topics broached during this decade have clearly been left out on other grounds. One example is *Dushu*'s very influential discussion on Che Guevara. In 1998 the journal published a commemoration of Che by the Latin Americanist, Suo Sa, which was the direct inspiration for a play by Huang Jisu and Zhang Guangtian, performed in 2000. Both Suo Sa's article and the *Che Guevara* play provoked intense debate among the Chinese intelligentsia: some considered this a retrogressive evocation of a revolutionary past that had been correctly eschewed by contemporary China; for others, it was a welcome revindication of the struggle for liberation. *Dushu* published several articles from different standpoints, debating the implications of this political symbol within the current context. It would have been very useful to have included these texts in the *Essentials of Dushu*, either in 'Reconstructing Our Image of the World', or in 'A Compelling Gaze'. They provide a good picture of how Chinese intellectuals view the country's revolutionary legacy and the contemporary shift away from it. The editors may have had their own concerns, political or technical, on this subject; but from a reader's perspective, these articles would certainly have added to the value of the selection.

Other politically sensitive pieces have also been left out, including the most controversial article published during this period, 'Writing History: Gao Village', by the sociologist Gao Mobo. The text explored the impact of the Cultural Revolution on the village's development and posed the question: who is dominating the narrative of the Cultural Revolution? *Dushu* published the piece with the aim of opening up plural perspectives on the GPCR and expected to create some debate. But 'Gao Village' was seen as challenging the political consensus between intellectuals and party bureaucrats since the 1980s that the Cultural Revolution had been a complete disaster. Ironically, it was not bureaucrats but liberal intellectuals who first detected a dangerous whiff, and who wrote, not to criticize Gao's scholarship, but to charge him with 'political incorrectness'.[12] Bureaucratic censors then intervened to forbid further discussion on the topic in *Dushu*. The clear implication is that it was impossible for 'Gao Village' to be included in the *Essentials* collection: the legitimacy of the market-reform era is, to a perhaps surprisingly large extent, based on a negative verdict on the Cultural Revolution; apparently, even a mildly positive picture of that period may seriously threaten to undermine it.

Critical context

Despite these shortcomings, the six-volume *Essentials of Dushu* is still a remarkable collection. The thematic arrangement allows these books to present a more orderly reflection of the journal's intellectual and political orientation during this period. While the authors come from a variety of different political viewpoints, the editors' response to China's current path of development is apparent from the overall agenda. For those who cling to a belief in the virtues of free-market modernization (or its variants), however, the questions that *Dushu* raises inevitably cause offence: within the journal's ambit, the codified criteria of modernization fall apart. Instead of the global market, freedom, democracy, human rights and the sciences going hand in hand, there can be serious conflicts of interest between them. The unitary path of modernization, modelled on the experiences of the West, is no longer viewed as the appropriate prescription for China's pathology. In the 1980s, intellectuals often used this model to criticize both the stagnation of the Chinese Empire and the destructive violence of the Revolution; but such a critique was generally marginalized in *Dushu* under Wang and Huang. The focus shifted to reflections on imperialism, colonialism, the socio-political conditions of the market, and the dynamism of Chinese history. For those who still hold fast to the old consensus, it has been pretty unpleasant to recognize that *Dushu*'s agenda-setting power was no longer in their hands.

With this background in mind, it is not difficult to understand why some intellectuals celebrated the end of *Dushu*'s 'Wang and Huang era'. Some have openly charged Wang with being against modernization and therefore a 'reactionary', who led *Dushu* in the wrong direction. Others, aware

---

[12] See the newspaper, *Nanfang Zhoumo* (Southern Weekend), 29 March 2001.

that modernization theory is an outdated paradigm even in the West, expressed their discontent more indirectly, on non-political grounds: *Dushu* under Wang and Huang has deviated from its elegant prose tradition and become too obscure to read; it is no longer the 'common space' or 'spiritual home' for the whole intelligentsia. To what extent is this true? As noted, it is the fifth volume, 'Not Only for Commemoration', that contains the most elegantly crafted literary pieces. There is much fine writing in the other volumes, too, signalling the editors' intention to maintain *Dushu*'s past style. However, the substance of some of these articles means that they can hardly avoid using the vocabulary necessary to respond to contemporary social, economic and political problems. Unlike the memoirs, these pieces tend to be analytical, and are often quite theoretical.

Again, this change in style needs to be understood with reference to the disciplinary differentiation that has taken place in China over the past decade. In the 1980s, intellectuals read all kinds of books without much consciousness of disciplinary boundaries; by the 1990s, the latter could no longer be ignored. Compared to literature, the new social sciences appeared to have a much higher knowledge threshold: the language of economics can be forbidding to a lay reader and there were many newly translated terms. Consequently, it has been hard to maintain the same level of literary elegance. In the recent debate, critics of Wang and Huang have interpreted this stylistic difference as symptomatic of the two editors' break from *Dushu*'s classical prose tradition. In fact, the complaint about readability was first made in the mid-1980s, when *Dushu* began to introduce Western theories. To keep up with the rapid intellectual changes of the time inevitably taxed old reading habits. But there is also the undeniable factor of generational difference: most intellectuals of Wang and Huang's generation did not receive a systematic education in the Chinese classics, which had been abolished after 1949. Some older intellectuals, like Fei Xiaotong, attended universities in the West, but because they had a thorough training in the classics before they went overseas, they were still able to write in elegant Chinese. The younger generation does not have that background to counterbalance the sudden influence of Western languages. But this is a structural constraint, within which the editors are obliged to labour. On the evidence of these volumes, it seems more accurate to say that Wang and Huang tried their best to make the journal more readable without lapsing into a populist style. *Dushu* rarely publishes highly specialized research papers, and encourages scholars to write in ways that will be comprehensible to the general reader. Analytical articles tend to be balanced by memoirs or other short pieces.

Quietism?

A further form of criticism has also been voiced by liberal Chinese intellectuals, most forthrightly by those outside the PRC: that although *Dushu* has taken a strong line against the CCP's inegalitarian neo-liberal economic policies, the journal has been much more cautious in advancing a political critique of the repressive character of the government. From the perspective of these critics, the first task of the intelligentsia should be to fight for intellectual autonomy from the regime. Unfortunately, while all may agree in principle on the desirability of such autonomy, even some of those now calling for it still seem to have the regime-centred mentality of inviting the bureaucracy to strike down their intellectual opponents. *Dushu* appears to have been a victim of this type of approach.

On the broader question at stake, it is quite true that Wang and Huang's editorship was in some respects politically cautious: the exclusions—Che, 'Gao Village'—from *The Essentials of Dushu*, noted above, are further illustrations of this. However, it would be wrong to say that Wang and Huang's *Dushu* has played no part in the critique of autocracy. The powerful liberal critic Qin Hui, for example (interviewed in NLR 20), has been an active contributor to the journal under their editorship and his work is included in the selection, as are texts by prominent liberals such as Qian Liqun (a historian of Chinese literature), He Qinglian (a reporter, now a political exile), Xu Ben (a US-based writer working on Hannah Arendt) and the late Li Shenzhi. After Wang and Huang's dismissal, Qian Liqun announced his regret in a symposium and called for intellectuals to unite in the struggle for free speech.

To summarize here inevitably involves flattening a highly variegated intellectual landscape: there are many subtleties and overlaps at play in this debate, which happily far exceeds the 'new left versus liberalism' label applied to it in the late 1990s. But it would be fair to say that Wang and Huang's *Dushu* has focused principally on exposing the political-economic logic of the alliance between capital and the oppressive-developmentalist state. Many of the journal's critics believe that the state is problematic, but capital is fine. From their perspective, therefore, *Dushu* has criticized capital too much, the state too little; this is the source of that line of argument.

The notion that *Dushu* was once known as the 'common home' for the entire Chinese intelligentsia is also a recent construction. As noted above, in the 1980s, *Dushu* was not the only platform for discussion, and quite a few other journals were equally influential. But here again, the relationship of the intelligentsia to changes in the wider society has to be taken into account. The 1980s consensus on modernization has broken down, and *Dushu* can no longer be based upon it. To reiterate: the journal did continue to publish articles by authors of different persuasions, including the free-market economists who answered He Qinglian's charges. The point that rankles among such critics, perhaps, is not that pro-market writers cannot be published in *Dushu*, but rather that over the past decade they have not been able to set its agenda.

A questioning voice

One might argue that Wang and Huang could have done more to accommodate the taste of those who held fast to the previous consensus. Nevertheless, it is doubtful that *Dushu* would have been able to maintain the image of a 'golden age' without sacrificing its critical quality, in the context of the wider intellectual polarization. For the past ideological consensus relied upon some irretrievable conditions: first, the unprecedented unity between Party bureaucrats and intellectuals brought about by the fresh memories of the Cultural Revolution; second, the undifferentiated interest structure of Chinese society. Today, a large section of the workers and peasants who have been marginalized by China's current path would themselves no longer subscribe to this ideological consensus. In this context, for *Dushu* to continue to operate according to 1980s values would inevitably mean losing sight of contemporary changes. It is in this situation that *Dushu* has chosen not to maintain the impossible 'unity' of the intellectual class, but to raise new questions for the whole society.

In fact, many of the issues *Dushu* has raised have become matters of common concern and even influenced public policy. The 'efficiency first' doctrine was officially revised in 2004, and sustainable development was given greater formal salience under the party's new slogan, 'scientific development'. Expenditure on health and social security has been increased, as have budgets for rural infrastructure; agricultural tax has been abolished. This is not to say that the growth in social disparities has been curbed, let alone halted. In many instances, local governments resist or sabotage social policies; for these officials, GDP growth is the most important indicator for their promotion through the bureaucratic system. This turns local government into a profiteering machine. Although top leaders may want to change this, many vested interest groups have come into being in local society, where administrative power and capital go hand in hand. In this situation, social policies can at the most ameliorate the ills of the development path but cannot cure them. Nevertheless, it would be fair to say that the dangers of social inequality have been more widely recognized, and the former priests of the 'efficiency first' doctrine are no longer considered unassailable. In Chinese cyberspace, neo-liberals are fiercely charged with having mismanaged reforms, resulting in enormous social inequality. The glowing image of the capitalist global market and political order has been brought into question, especially since China's exports have encountered trade protectionism in the US and Europe in recent years. This has enabled many people to see that the world is not flat. Liberals now tend to clarify that they are not neo-liberals, and tend to take social justice more seriously in what they write. It would be wrong to ignore the impact of *Dushu*'s persistent work on all this.

But these changes do not heal the existing cleavage in the Chinese intelligentsia; this is, if anything, deepening. The form of Wang and Huang's dismissal may seem to be non-political; but strictly speaking, it is a depoliticized political process. The technical pretext used by the SDX Publishing Company does not hold water. The true reason must lie elsewhere. Most intellectuals in China have no difficulty in figuring out the political implication of this sudden change. As a state-owned enterprise, SDX is affiliated to the China Publishing Group, which is further supervised by the Central Propaganda Department of the CCP. Bureaucrats have a strong incentive to tame this 'trouble-making' journal; for although *Dushu*'s style is very moderate, the ideas it spreads could potentially be dangerous, and neo-liberal intellectuals have long spoken ill of it. We may never know what was going on in the black box; but even before SDX made the announcement, liberal newspapers had spread the news that *Dushu* was to replace its chief editors, and some of its critics had already begun to celebrate their victory.

Unexpectedly, then, this six-volume collection marks the end of *Dushu*'s 'Wang and Huang era'. What course the journal will now take remains to be seen. Initially, it seemed to stay on the same track for several months after Wang and Huang's departure. More substantial changes look to have appeared with the January 2008 issue, which opens with a 'Call for a Market Economy with the Rule of Law'. It seems unlikely that the previous editors would have used an official political slogan of this type as the title for an intellectual discussion. The *Essentials of Dushu* collection remains a window through which the world can see China's social upheavals during this eventful decade, and situate the intelligentsia's thinking within its historical context. The period has witnessed a dramatic reversal: the thinkers and writers once united by an aspiration for modernization are now divided by the bitter process of reform and development. In the face of these painful splits, some cannot help but look back to the unity of the 1980s for consolation. For these distracted minds, the past looks increasingly like a golden age. In an era of nostalgia, the *Essentials of Dushu, 1996–2005* makes for sober reading: the 'golden age' is all the more irretrievably lost, for now even the myth that it was based on dissolves into the air. For China's intellectuals, now is the time to stand on one's own two feet and struggle bravely for recognition.

读书

2007 4 April

D U S H U

The cover of *Dushu*'s April 2007 issue. *Contents: Xu Baoqiang, 'The Nature of Free Competition'; Zhou Bo, 'Design for the People'; Su Li, 'Judicial Insights in Ancient China'; Liu Xiaofeng, 'Warrior Family Precepts in Japan'; Li Minghuan, 'Women in Migration'; Kong Gaofeng, 'The 21st Century: Still American?'; Su Guoxun, 'Reflections on Sociology Classics'.*

Torture and Democracy

Darius Rejali

"*Torture and Democracy* brings the fact of torture straight home to democratic societies—societies that are the most reluctant to acknowledge the presence of torture in their midst."
—Edward Peters, author of *Torture*

Cloth $39.50 978-0-691-11422-4

Democracy Incorporated

Managed Democracy and the Specter of Inverted Totalitarianism

Sheldon S. Wolin

"There is nothing like this book. It is a major, potentially revolutionary contribution to political thought."
—Anne Norton, author of *Leo Strauss and the Politics of American Empire*

Cloth $29.95 978-0-691-13566-3 Due May

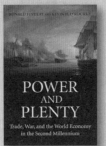

Power and Plenty

Trade, War, and the World Economy in the Second Millennium

Ronald Findlay & Kevin H. O'Rourke

"An excellent reference book for anyone wanting a better understanding of economic developments in the last millennium."—*Economist*

The Princeton Economic History of the Western World
Joel Mokyr, Series Editor
Cloth $39.50 978-0-691-11854-3

The Spaces of the Modern City

Imaginaries, Politics, and Everyday Life

Edited by Gyan Prakash & Kevin M. Kruse

"Combining conceptual sophistication with rich historical studies, [this] book moves beyond familiar reference points in debates about urban modernity."
—David Pinder, Queen Mary, University of London

Paper $24.95 978-0-691-13343-0
Cloth $65.00 978-0-691-13339-3

 PRINCETON UNIVERSITY PRESS

ALAIN BADIOU

THE COMMUNIST HYPOTHESIS

T HERE WAS A tangible sense of depression in the air in France in the aftermath of Sarkozy's victory.[1] It is often said that unexpected blows are the worst, but expected ones sometimes prove debilitating in a different way. It can be oddly dispiriting when an election is won by the candidate who has led in the opinion polls from the start, just as when the favourite horse wins the race; anyone with the slightest feeling for a wager, a risk, an exception or a rupture would rather see an outsider upset the odds. Yet it could hardly have been the bare fact of Nicolas Sarkozy as President that seemed to come as such a disorientating blow to the French left in the aftermath of May 2007. Something else was at stake—some complex of factors for which 'Sarkozy' is merely a name. How should it be understood?

An initial factor was the way in which the outcome affirmed the manifest powerlessness of any genuinely emancipatory programme within the electoral system: preferences are duly recorded, in the passive manner of a seismograph, but the process is one that by its nature excludes any embodiments of dissenting political will. A second component of the left's depressive disorientation after May 2007 was an overwhelming bout of historical nostalgia. The political order that emerged from World War Two in France—with its unambiguous referents of 'left' and 'right', and its consensus, shared by Gaullists and Communists alike, on the balance-sheet of the Occupation, Resistance and Liberation—has now collapsed. This is one reason for Sarkozy's ostentatious dinners, yachting holidays and so on—a way of saying that the left no longer frightens anyone: *Vivent les riches*, and to hell with the poor. Understandably, this may fill the sincere souls of the left with nostalgia for the good old days— Mitterrand, De Gaulle, Marchais, even Chirac, Gaullism's Brezhnev, who knew that to do nothing was the easiest way to let the system die.

Sarkozy has now finally finished off the cadaverous form of Gaullism over which Chirac presided. The Socialists' collapse had already been antici-pated in the rout of Jospin in the presidential elections of 2002 (and still more by the disastrous decision to embrace Chirac in the second round). The present decomposition of the Socialist Party, however, is not just a matter of its political poverty, apparent now for many years, nor of the actual size of the vote—47 per cent is not much worse than its other recent scores. Rather, the election of Sarkozy appears to have struck a blow to the entire symbolic structuring of French political life: the system of orienta-tion itself has suffered a defeat. An important symptom of the resulting disorientation is the number of former Socialist placemen rushing to take up appointments under Sarkozy, the centre-left opinion-makers singing his praises; the rats have fled the sinking ship in impressive numbers. The underlying rationale is, of course, that of the single party: since all accept the logic of the existing capitalist order, market economy and so forth, why maintain the fiction of opposing parties?

A third component of the contemporary disorientation arose from the outcome of the electoral conflict itself. I have characterized the 2007 presidential elections—pitting Sarkozy against Royal—as the clash of two types of fear. The first is the fear felt by the privileged, alarmed that their position may be assailable. In France this manifests itself as fear of foreigners, workers, youth from the *banlieue*, Muslims, black Africans. Essentially conservative, it creates a longing for a protective master, even one who oppresses and impoverishes you further. The current embodi-ment of this figure is, of course, the over-stimulated police chief: Sarkozy. In electoral terms, this is contested not by a resounding affirmation of self-determining heterogeneity, but by the fear of this fear: a fear, too, of the cop figure, whom the petit-bourgeois socialist voter neither knows nor likes. This 'fear of the fear' is a secondary, derivative emotion, whose content—beyond the sentiment itself—is barely detectable; the Royal camp had no concept of any alliance with the excluded or oppressed; the most it could envisage was to reap the dubious benefits of fear. For both sides, a total consensus reigned on Palestine, Iran, Afghanistan (where French forces are fighting), Lebanon (ditto), Africa (swarming with French military 'administrators'). Public discussion of alternatives on these issues was on neither party's agenda.

[1] This is an edited extract from *De quoi Sarkozy est-il le nom?*, *Circonstances, 4*, Nouvelles Editions Lignes, Paris 2007; to be published in English by Verso as *What Do We Mean When We Say 'Sarkozy'?* in 2008.

The conflict between the primary fear and the 'fear of the fear' was settled in favour of the former. There was a visceral reflex in play here, very
apparent in the faces of those partying over Sarkozy's victory. For those
in the grip of the 'fear of the fear' there was a corresponding negative
reflex, flinching from the result: this was the third component of 2007's
depressive disorientation. We should not underestimate the role of what
Althusser called the 'ideological state apparatus'—increasingly through
the media, with the press now playing a more sophisticated part than TV
and radio—in formulating and mobilizing such collective sentiments.
Within the electoral process there has, it seems, been a weakening of
the real; a process even further advanced with regard to the secondary
'fear of the fear' than with the primitive, reactionary one. We react, after
all, to a real situation, whereas the 'fear of the fear' merely takes fright at
the scale of that reaction, and is thus at a still further remove from reality. The vacuity of this position manifested itself perfectly in the empty
exaltations of Ségolène Royal.

Electoralism and the state

If we posit a definition of politics as 'collective action, organized by certain principles, that aims to unfold the consequences of a new possibility
which is currently repressed by the dominant order', then we would
have to conclude that the electoral mechanism is an essentially apoliti-
cal procedure. This can be seen in the gulf between the massive formal
imperative to vote and the free-floating, if not non-existent nature of
political or ideological convictions. It is good to vote, to give a form to my
fears; but it is hard to believe that what I am voting *for* is a good thing in
itself. This is not to say that the electoral-democratic system is repressive
per se; rather, that the electoral process is incorporated into a state form,
that of capitalo-parliamentarianism, appropriate for the maintenance of
the established order, and consequently serves a conservative function.
This creates a further feeling of powerlessness: if ordinary citizens have
no handle on state decision-making save the vote, it is hard to see what
way forward there could be for an emancipatory politics.

If the electoral mechanism is not a political but a state procedure, what
does it achieve? Drawing on the lessons of 2007, one effect is to incor-
porate both the fear and the 'fear of the fear' into the state—to invest
the state with these mass-subjective elements, the better to legitimate
it as an object of fear in its own right, equipped for terror and coercion.

For the world horizon of democracy is increasingly defined by war. The West is engaged on an expanding number of fronts: the maintenance of the existing order with its gigantic disparities has an irreducible military component; the duality of the worlds of rich and poor can only be sustained by force. This creates a particular dialectic of war and fear. Our governments explain that they are waging war abroad in order to protect us from it at home. If Western troops do not hunt down the terrorists in Afghanistan or Chechnya, they will come over here to organize the resentful rabble outcasts.

Strategic neo-Pétainism

In France, this alliance of fear and war has classically gone by the name of Pétainism. The mass ideology of Pétainism—responsible for its widespread success between 1940 and 1944—rested in part on the fear generated by the First World War: Marshal Pétain would protect France from the disastrous effects of the Second, by keeping well out of it. In the Marshal's own words, it was necessary to be more afraid of war than of defeat. The vast majority of the French accepted the relative tranquillity of a consensual defeat and most got off fairly lightly during the War, compared to the Russians or even the English. The analogous project today is based on the belief that the French need simply to accept the laws of the us-led world model and all will be well: France will be protected from the disastrous effects of war and global disparity. This form of neo-Pétainism as a mass ideology is effectively on offer from both parties today. In what follows, I will argue that it is a key analytical element in understanding the disorientation that goes by the name of 'Sarkozy'; to grasp the latter in its overall dimension, its historicity and intelligibility, requires us to go back to what I will call its Pétainist 'transcendental'.[2]

I am not saying, of course, that circumstances today resemble the defeat of 1940, or that Sarkozy resembles Pétain. The point is a more formal one: that the unconscious national-historical roots of that which goes by the name of Sarkozy are to be found in this Pétainist configuration, in which the disorientation itself is solemnly enacted from the

---

[2] See my *Logiques des mondes*, Paris 2006 for a full development of the concept of 'transcendentals' and their function, which is to govern the order of appearance of multiplicities within a world.

summit of the state, and presented as a historical turning-point. This matrix has been a recurring pattern in French history. It goes back to the Restoration of 1815 when a post-Revolutionary government, eagerly supported by émigrés and opportunists, was brought back in the foreigners' baggage-train and declared, with the consent of a worn-out population, that it would restore public morality and order. In 1940, military defeat once again served as the context for the disorientating reversal of the real content of state action: the Vichy government spoke incessantly of the 'nation', yet was installed by the German Occupation; the most corrupt of oligarchs were to lead the country out of moral crisis; Pétain himself, an ageing general in the service of property, would be the embodiment of national rebirth.

Numerous aspects of this neo-Pétainist tradition are in evidence today. Typically, capitulation and servility are presented as invention and regeneration. These were central themes of Sarkozy's campaign: the Mayor of Neuilly would transform the French economy and put the country back to work. The real content, of course, is a politics of continuous obedience to the demands of high finance, in the name of national renewal. A second characteristic is that of decline and 'moral crisis', which justifies the repressive measures taken in the name of regeneration. Morality is invoked, as so often, in place of politics and against any popular mobilization. Appeal is made instead to the virtues of hard work, discipline, the family: 'merit should be rewarded'. This typical displacement of politics by morality has been prepared, from the 1970s 'new philosophers' onwards, by all who have laboured to 'moralize' historical judgement. The object is in reality political: to maintain that national decline has nothing to do with the high servants of capital but is the fault of certain ill-intentioned elements of the population—currently, foreign workers and young people from the *banlieue*.

A third characteristic of neo-Pétainism is the paradigmatic function of foreign experience. The example of correction always comes from abroad, from countries that have long overcome their moral crises. For Pétain, the shining examples were Mussolini's Italy, Hitler's Germany and Franco's Spain: leaders who had put their countries back on their feet. The political aesthetic is that of imitation: like Plato's demiurge, the state must shape society with its eyes fixed on foreign models. Today, of course, the examples are Bush's America and Blair's Britain.

A fourth characteristic is the notion that the source of the current crisis lies in a disastrous past event. For the proto-Pétainism of the 1815
Restoration, this was of course the Revolution and the beheading of the
King. For Pétain himself in 1940 it was the Popular Front, the Blum
government and above all the great strikes and factory occupations of
1936. The possessing classes far preferred the German Occupation to
the fear which these disorders had provoked. For Sarkozy, the evils of
May 68—forty years ago—have been constantly invoked as the cause
of the current 'crisis of values'. Neo-Pétainism provides a usefully simplified reading of history that links a negative event, generally with a
working-class or popular structure, and a positive one, with a military
or state structure, as a solution to the first. The arc between 1968 and
2007 can thus be offered as a source of legitimacy for the Sarkozy government, as the historic actor that will finally embark on the correction
needed in the wake of the inaugural damaging event. Finally, there is the
element of racism. Under Pétain this was brutally explicit: getting rid of
the Jews. Today it is voiced in a more insinuating fashion: 'we are not an
inferior race'—the implication being, 'unlike others'; 'the true French
need not doubt the legitimacy of their country's actions'—in Algeria
and elsewhere. In the light of these criteria, we can therefore point: the
disorientation that goes by the name of 'Sarkozy' may be analysed as the
latest manifestation of the Pétainist transcendental.

The spectre

At first sight there may seem something strange about the new President's
insistence that the solution to the country's moral crisis, the goal of his
'renewal' process, was 'to do away with May 68, once and for all'. Most
of us were under the impression that it was long gone anyway. What is
haunting the regime, under the name of May 68? We can only assume
that it is the 'spectre of communism', in one of its last real manifestations. He would say (to give a Sarkozian prosopopoeia): 'We refuse to be
haunted by anything at all. It is not enough that empirical communism
has disappeared. We want all possible forms of it banished. Even the
hypothesis of communism—generic name of our defeat—must become
unmentionable.'

What is the communist hypothesis? In its generic sense, given in its
canonic *Manifesto*, 'communist' means, first, that the logic of class—
the fundamental subordination of labour to a dominant class, the

arrangement that has persisted since Antiquity—is not inevitable; it can be overcome. The communist hypothesis is that a different collective organization is practicable, one that will eliminate the inequality of wealth and even the division of labour. The private appropriation of massive fortunes and their transmission by inheritance will disappear. The existence of a coercive state, separate from civil society, will no longer appear a necessity: a long process of reorganization based on a free association of producers will see it withering away.

'Communism' as such denotes only this very general set of intellectual representations. It is what Kant called an Idea, with a regulatory function, rather than a programme. It is foolish to call such communist principles utopian; in the sense that I have defined them here they are intellectual patterns, always actualized in a different fashion. As a pure Idea of equality, the communist hypothesis has no doubt existed since the beginnings of the state. As soon as mass action opposes state coercion in the name of egalitarian justice, rudiments or fragments of the hypothesis start to appear. Popular revolts—the slaves led by Spartacus, the peasants led by Müntzer—might be identified as practical examples of this 'communist invariant'. With the French Revolution, the communist hypothesis then inaugurates the epoch of political modernity.

What remains is to determine the point at which we now find ourselves in the history of the communist hypothesis. A fresco of the modern period would show two great sequences in its development, with a forty-year gap between them. The first is that of the setting in place of the communist hypothesis; the second, of preliminary attempts at its realization. The first sequence runs from the French Revolution to the Paris Commune; let us say, 1792 to 1871. It links the popular mass movement to the seizure of power, through the insurrectional overthrow of the existing order; this revolution will abolish the old forms of society and install 'the community of equals'. In the course of the century, the formless popular movement made up of townsfolk, artisans and students came increasingly under the leadership of the working class. The sequence culminated in the striking novelty—and radical defeat—of the Paris Commune. For the Commune demonstrated both the extraordinary energy of this combination of popular movement, working-class leadership and armed insurrection, and its limits: the *communards* could neither establish the revolution on a national footing nor defend it against the foreign-backed forces of the counter-revolution.

The second sequence of the communist hypothesis runs from 1917 to 1976: from the Bolshevik Revolution to the end of the Cultural Revolution and the militant upsurge throughout the world during the years 1966–75. It was dominated by the question: how to win? How to hold out—unlike the Paris Commune—against the armed reaction of the possessing classes; how to organize the new power so as to protect it against the onslaught of its enemies? It was no longer a question of for-mulating and testing the communist hypothesis, but of realizing it: what the 19th century had dreamt, the 20th would accomplish. The obses-sion with victory, centred around questions of organization, found its principal expression in the 'iron discipline' of the communist party—the characteristic construction of the second sequence of the hypothesis. The party effectively solved the question inherited from the first sequence: the revolution prevailed, either through insurrection or prolonged popu-lar war, in Russia, China, Czechoslovakia, Korea, Vietnam, Cuba, and succeeded in establishing a new order.

But the second sequence in turn created a further problem, which it could not solve using the methods it had developed in response to the problems of the first. The party had been an appropriate tool for the overthrow of weakened reactionary regimes, but it proved ill-adapted for the construction of the 'dictatorship of the proletariat' in the sense that Marx had intended—that is, a temporary state, organizing the transition to the non-state: its dialectical 'withering away'. Instead, the party-state developed into a new form of authoritarianism. Some of these regimes made real strides in education, public health, the valorization of labour, and so on; and they provided an international constraint on the arrogance of the imperialist powers. However, the statist principle in itself proved corrupt and, in the long run, ineffective. Police coercion could not save the 'socialist' state from internal bureaucratic inertia; and within fifty years it was clear that it would never prevail in the fero-cious competition imposed by its capitalist adversaries. The last great convulsions of the second sequence—the Cultural Revolution and May 68, in its broadest sense—can be understood as attempts to deal with the inadequacy of the party.

Interludes

Between the end of the first sequence and the beginning of the second there was a forty-year interval during which the communist hypothesis

was declared to be untenable: the decades from 1871 to 1914 saw imperialism triumphant across the globe. Since the second sequence came
to an end in the 1970s we have been in another such interval, with the
adversary in the ascendant once more. What is at stake in these circumstances is the eventual opening of a new sequence of the communist
hypothesis. But it is clear that this will not be—cannot be—the continuation of the second one. Marxism, the workers' movement, mass
democracy, Leninism, the party of the proletariat, the socialist state—all
the inventions of the 20th century—are not really useful to us any more.
At the theoretical level they certainly deserve further study and consideration; but at the level of practical politics they have become unworkable.
The second sequence is over and it is pointless to try to restore it.

At this point, during an interval dominated by the enemy, when new
experiments are tightly circumscribed, it is not possible to say with cer-
tainty what the character of the third sequence will be. But the general
direction seems discernible: it will involve a new relation between the
political movement and the level of the ideological—one that was prefig-
ured in the expression 'cultural revolution' or in the May 68 notion of a
'revolution of the mind'. We will still retain the theoretical and historical
lessons that issued from the first sequence, and the centrality of victory
that issued from the second. But the solution will be neither the formless, or multi-form, popular movement inspired by the intelligence of the
multitude—as Negri and the alter-globalists believe—nor the renewed
and democratized mass communist party, as some of the Trotskyists
and Maoists hope. The (19th-century) movement and the (20th-century)
party were specific modes of the communist hypothesis; it is no longer
possible to return to them. Instead, after the negative experiences of the
'socialist' states and the ambiguous lessons of the Cultural Revolution
and May 68, our task is to bring the communist hypothesis into existence in another mode, to help it emerge within new forms of political
experience. This is why our work is so complicated, so experimental.
We must focus on its conditions of existence, rather than just improv-
ing its methods. We need to re-install the communist hypothesis—the
proposition that the subordination of labour to the dominant class is not
inevitable—within the ideological sphere.

What might this involve? Experimentally, we might conceive of finding
a point that would stand outside the temporality of the dominant order
and what Lacan once called 'the service of wealth'. Any point, so long

as it is in formal opposition to such service, and offers the discipline of a universal truth. One such might be the declaration: 'There is only one world'. What would this imply? Contemporary capitalism boasts, of course, that it has created a global order; its opponents too speak of 'alter-globalization'. Essentially, they propose a definition of politics as a practical means of moving from the world as it is to the world as we would wish it to be. But does a single world of human subjects exist? The 'one world' of globalization is solely one of things—objects for sale—and monetary signs: the world market as foreseen by Marx. The overwhelming majority of the population have at best restricted access to this world. They are locked out, often literally so.

The fall of the Berlin Wall was supposed to signal the advent of the single world of freedom and democracy. Twenty years later, it is clear that the world's wall has simply shifted: instead of separating East and West it now divides the rich capitalist North from the poor and devastated South. New walls are being constructed all over the world: between Palestinians and Israelis, between Mexico and the United States, between Africa and the Spanish enclaves, between the pleasures of wealth and the desires of the poor, whether they be peasants in villages or urban dwellers in *favelas, banlieues*, estates, hostels, squats and shantytowns. The price of the supposedly unified world of capital is the brutal division of human existence into regions separated by police dogs, bureaucratic controls, naval patrols, barbed wire and expulsions. The 'problem of immigration' is, in reality, the fact that the conditions faced by workers from other countries provide living proof that—in human terms—the 'unified world' of globalization is a sham.

A *performative unity*

The political problem, then, has to be reversed. We cannot start from an analytic agreement on the existence of the world and proceed to normative action with regard to its characteristics. The disagreement is not over qualities but over existence. Confronted with the artificial and murderous division of the world into two—a disjunction named by the very term, 'the West'—we must affirm the existence of the single world right from the start, as axiom and principle. The simple phrase, 'there is only one world', is not an objective conclusion. It is performative: we are deciding that this is how it is for us. Faithful to this point, it is then a question of elucidating the consequences that follow from this simple declaration.

A first consequence is the recognition that all belong to the same world as myself: the African worker I see in the restaurant kitchen, the Moroccan I see digging a hole in the road, the veiled woman looking after children in a park. That is where we reverse the dominant idea of the world united by objects and signs, to make a unity in terms of living, acting beings, here and now. These people, different from me in terms of language, clothes, religion, food, education, exist exactly as I do myself; since they exist like me, I can discuss with them—and, as with anyone else, we can agree and disagree about things. But on the precondition that they and I exist in the same world.

At this point, the objection about cultural difference will be raised: 'our' world is made up of those who accept 'our' values—democracy, respect for women, human rights. Those whose culture is contrary to this are not really part of the same world; if they want to join it they have to share our values, to 'integrate'. As Sarkozy put it: 'If foreigners want to remain in France, they have to love France; otherwise, they should leave.' But to place conditions is already to have abandoned the principle, 'there is only one world of living men and women'. It may be said that we need to take the laws of each country into account. Indeed; but a law does not set a precondition for belonging to the world. It is simply a provisional rule that exists in a particular region of the single world. And no one is asked to love a law, simply to obey it. The single world of living women and men may well have laws; what it cannot have is subjective or 'cultural' preconditions for existence within it—to demand that you have to be like everyone else. The single world is precisely the place where an unlimited set of differences exist. Philosophically, far from casting doubt on the unity of the world, these differences are its principle of existence.

The question then arises whether anything governs these unlimited differences. There may well be only one world, but does that mean that being French, or a Moroccan living in France, or Muslim in a country of Christian traditions, is nothing? Or should we see the persistence of such identities as an obstacle? The simplest definition of 'identity' is the series of characteristics and properties by which an individual or a group recognizes itself as its 'self'. But what is this 'self'? It is that which, across all the characteristic properties of identity, remains more or less invariant. It is possible, then, to say that an identity is the ensemble of properties that support an invariance. For example, the identity of an artist is that by which the invariance of his or her style can be recognized; homosexual identity is composed of everything bound up with the invariance of the possible object of desire; the identity of a foreign community in a country is that by which membership of this community can be recognized: language, gestures, dress, dietary habits, etc.

Defined in this way, by invariants, identity is doubly related to difference: on the one hand, identity is that which is different from the rest; on the other, it is that which does not become different, which is invariant. The affirmation of identity has two further aspects. The first form is negative. It consists of desperately maintaining that I am not the other. This is often indispensable, in the face of authoritarian demands for integration, for example. The Moroccan worker will forcefully affirm that his traditions and customs are not those of the petty-bourgeois European; he will even reinforce the characteristics of his religious or customary identity. The second involves the immanent development of identity within a new situation—rather like Nietzsche's famous maxim, 'become what you are'. The Moroccan worker does not abandon that which constitutes his individual identity, whether socially or in the family; but he will gradually adapt all this, in a creative fashion, to the place in which he finds himself. He will thus invent what he is—a Moroccan worker in Paris—not through any internal rupture, but by an expansion of identity.

The political consequences of the axiom, 'there is only one world', will work to consolidate what is universal in identities. An example—a local experiment—would be a meeting held recently in Paris, where undocumented workers and French nationals came together to demand the abolition of persecutory laws, police raids and expulsions; to demand that foreign workers be recognized simply in terms of their presence: that no one is illegal; all demands that are very natural for people who are basically in the same existential situation—people of the same world.

Time and courage

'In such great misfortune, what remains to you?' Corneille's Medea is asked by her confidante. 'Myself! Myself, I say, and it is enough', comes the reply. What Medea retains is the courage to decide her own fate; and courage, I would suggest, is the principal virtue in face of the disorientation of our own times. Lacan also raises the issue in discussing the analytical cure for depressive debility: should this not end in grand dialectical discussions on courage and justice, on the model of Plato's dialogues? In the famous 'Dialogue on Courage', General Laches, questioned by Socrates, replies: 'Courage is when I see the enemy and run towards him to engage him in a fight.' Socrates is not particularly satisfied with this, of course, and gently takes the General to task: 'It's a good example of courage, but an example is not a definition.' Running the same risks as General Laches, I will give my definition.

First, I would retain the status of courage as a virtue—that is, not an innate disposition, but something that constructs itself, and which one constructs, in practice. Courage, then, is the virtue which manifests itself through endurance in the impossible. This is not simply a matter of a momentary encounter with the impossible: that would be heroism, not courage. Heroism has always been represented not as a virtue but as a posture: as the moment when one turns to meet the impossible face to face. The virtue of courage constructs itself through endurance within the impossible; time is its raw material. What takes courage is to operate in terms of a different *durée* to that imposed by the law of the world. The point we are seeking must be one that can connect to another order of time. Those imprisoned within the temporality assigned us by the dominant order will always be prone to exclaim, as so many Socialist Party henchmen have done, 'Twelve years of Chirac, and now we have to wait for another round of elections. Seventeen years; perhaps twenty-two; a whole lifetime!' At best, they will become depressed and disorientated; at worst, rats.

In many respects we are closer today to the questions of the 19th century than to the revolutionary history of the 20th. A wide variety of 19th-century phenomena are reappearing: vast zones of poverty, widening inequalities, politics dissolved into the 'service of wealth', the nihilism of large sections of the young, the servility of much of the intelligentsia; the cramped, besieged experimentalism of a few groups seeking ways to express the communist hypothesis . . . Which is no doubt why, as in the 19th century, it is not the victory of the hypothesis which is at stake today, but the conditions of its existence. This is our task, during the reactionary interlude that now prevails: through the combination of thought processes—always global, or universal, in character—and political experience, always local or singular, yet transmissible, to renew the existence of the communist hypothesis, in our consciousness and on the ground.

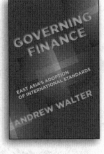

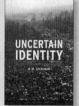

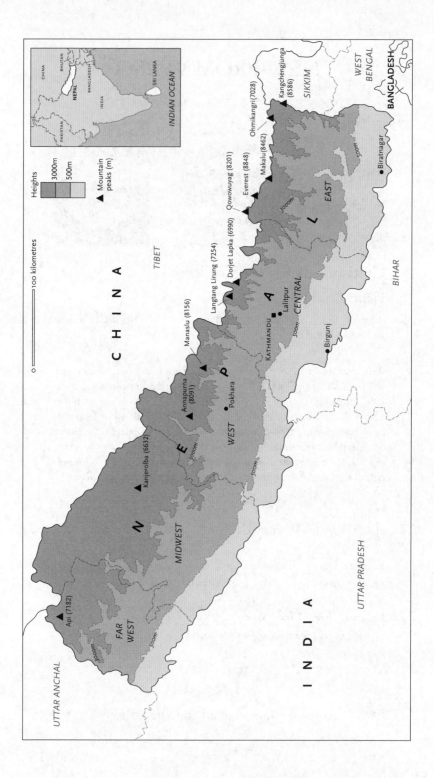

ACHIN VANAIK

THE NEW HIMALAYAN REPUBLIC

A WORLD-HISTORIC EVENT OCCURRED in a small South Asian country on 23 December 2007, when the toppling of the centuries-old Nepali monarchy and its replacement by a democratic federal republic was codified by the country's interim parliament.[1] The political force principally responsible for this achievement has been the Communist Party of Nepal (Maoist). Starting from the early 1990s the CPN-M had embarked, against all received wisdom, on a strategy of underground armed struggle which, within a decade, propelled it to the very forefront of Nepali politics. Militarily, it had fought to a stalemate—at the very least—the Royal Nepal Army. Politically, it had redefined the national agenda with its central demand for an elected Constituent Assembly, to draw up a constitution that would in turn ensure the formation of a new kind of Nepali state—republican, democratic, egalitarian, federal and secular.

In 2005, at the peak of its military influence, the CPN-M made a strategic turn to seek a permanent peace settlement and forge an alliance for democracy with Nepal's mainstream parliamentary parties, against the dictatorial rule of King Gyanendra. In so doing, it opened up a completely new phase in the turbulent political history of Nepal and paved the way for the remarkable mass upsurge of April 2006, known to Nepalis as the Second Democratic Revolution—Jan Andolan II. Beginning on April 6, with the declaration of a 4-day general strike and rally for democracy, the Jan Andolan turned into a 19-day uprising that brought over a million people into the streets of Kathmandu and the other cities, braving tear gas, baton charges, plastic bullets, arrests and, eventually, an 18-hour 'shoot-to-kill' curfew. The strike was soon declared indefinite and joined by shop-keepers, drivers, civil servants and even bankers, the cities soon running short of food, fuel and cash. The Royal Nepalese Army shot dead at least 15 protesters—by most estimates many more. Finally, faced with the threat of a 2-million-strong march on the Palace, King Gyanendra capitulated on April 24. The monarchy was stripped of its special executive powers and its very existence made subject to the rulings of a prospective Constituent Assembly.

Negotiations in the aftermath of the uprising have often been fraught. On the political front, an initial set of agreements between the Maoists and the new Interim Government, headed by the veteran Nepal Congress leader Girija Prasad Koirala, had laid out a roadmap for elections to the new Constituent Assembly, originally scheduled for June 2007. The Assembly was to have 497 seats, with 240 to be decided by a first-past-the-post constituency-based system, another 240 by proportional representation based on party lists, and the remaining 17 filled by 'eminences' nominated by the Cabinet. In the meantime, there would be an interim parliament where division of the total tally of 330 seats would approximate the proportions of the 1999 elections to the then lower house of 205 seats, with an extra allocation to the Maoists who had not stood in 1999. This meant over 100 seats for the Nepal Congress, the oldest bourgeois party, around 80 for the centre-left Communist Party of Nepal (Unified Marxist-Leninist), and the same number for the CPN-M.

On the military front, the Maoists' People's Liberation Army duly handed over 2,857 weapons to the UN Mission in Nepal on 7 March 2007, the Nepal Army having agreed to hand over an equal cache; each force would keep the sole key to its arms locker, which would be guarded by the UN. The joint agreement stipulated that the Nepal Army would remain in its barracks, and the combatants of the PLA would be confined to seven cantonments, where their upkeep was to be the responsibility of the Interim Government. Most importantly, it was agreed that a process of 'Security Sector Reform' or 'Democratization of the Army' would be initiated, which would integrate the soldiers and officers of the Nepal Army and the PLA.[2]

---

[1] This brings the number of monarchies recognized as UN states down to 27. I am greatly indebted to Anand Swaroop Verma and Pramod Kaphley for their practical help, without which this article could not have been written. I have benefited from their sound advice on many matters, but of course responsibility for the views presented here is mine alone.

[2] The Maoists have padded their camp numbers by sending in supporters otherwise struggling to subsist, as well as under-age fighters. There is an informal consensus that UN verification will weed out several thousand of these, leaving around 15,000 to be integrated. Security sector reform thus also entails provision of education and skills training, and for many, 'golden handshakes'.

On this basis, the CPN-M joined the Interim Government on 1 April 2007, expecting that this would bring them both domestic and international legitimacy. The message was driven home to Nepal's state bureaucracy that it had better come to terms with these new masters, and several European capitals were obliged to remove the Maoists from their 'terrorist' lists. But the general euphoria of the CPN-M in the immediate aftermath of Jan Andolan II gradually gave way to consternation as, with belated but accumulating force, the logic of electoral politics began to hit home. With full proportional representation, each of the main parties—the Maoists, the NC and the CPN-UML—might expect to get roughly a third of the seats in a Constituent Assembly election. Under the mixed electoral system to which the Maoists had initially given their consent, however, they were likely to come a poor third to their main rivals. With regard to the 240 (out of 480) elected seats that were due to be filled on a first-past-the-post constituency basis, the other two parties were amply endowed with what the Maoists lacked: well-funded campaign coffers, long-standing patronage structures and readily identifiable candidates. As the leading forces in the new Constituent Assembly, these two parties would be strongly placed to garner most of the credit for the republic that the Assembly would declare, and to shape the actual content of the new constitution and of future government policy. Maoist representation might be reduced to a sixth of the Assembly's seats. Understandably, this prospect caused deep dismay and anger within CPN-M ranks, especially among the sections that had always been unhappy with the 'strategic turn'.

On 18 September 2007 the Maoists pulled out of the Interim Government and threatened public agitation to back their call for a full proportional-representation voting system for all 480 elected seats in the Constituent Assembly, and for the Interim Government itself to declare the Republic of Nepal forthwith. These were cardinal demands, but went back on written commitments that the CPN-M leaders had already given. Unsurprisingly the CPN-M were widely accused in Nepal and abroad of irresponsibility and untrustworthiness, in seeking to derail a process that they had themselves endorsed once they realized that they might not achieve sufficient electoral support within the rules agreed.

But if on the surface this seems obvious enough, there is a deeper reality. In the transition from being an armed revolutionary 'outsider' to working within the established Nepali state framework, the Maoists have discovered grave unanticipated dilemmas caused not just by their own mistakes and arrogance, but by the duplicity and machinations of various forces opposed to them. In addition to their own-goal in agreeing to an unrepresentative voting system that could only benefit the established parties with well-oiled electoral machines, the key issue has been that of military reform. In the months following Jan Andolan II, Prime Minister Koirala adamantly refused to sack any of the RNA's top 25 generals, who bore responsibility not just for the April 2006 shootings but for thousands of civilian deaths during the civil war, and who were besides deeply compromised by their close association with the dictatorial King. The upshot is that although it was the Maoists, far more than any other force, that were responsible for the new and highly positive transformation of Nepal's political trajectory, it is likely that their gains will not be at all commensurate with their contribution. Their new demands were an attempt at least to narrow this gap.

How things came to such a pass, and where the Maoists go from here, however, are questions that must be situated in a wider understanding of Nepal's polity and economy, of the external forces at play, and of the country's extraordinarily complex internal patchwork of class, caste, linguistic and ethnic divisions. Nepal was never directly colonized, so its autocratic and highly conservative form of monarchical rule did not have to face the 'energy from below' of a rising national liberation movement during the colonial era. As a de facto tributary kingdom, first to the British Raj and then to post-Independence India, Nepal had no cause to undertake the reforms necessary to create the pre-conditions for a sovereign nation-state: a modern standing army, a centralized civil-service bureaucracy, a system of secular and unifying jurisprudence, country-wide taxation and infrastructural development aimed at creating a national market. It was, of course, the country's extreme underdevelopment that finally allowed a classic, peasant-based and Maoist-led 'revolutionary upsurge from below' to flourish, following a strategic path of countryside encircling the cities; moreover, the Maoist leaders were well aware that their project for a 'people's democracy' had to reckon with the fall of communism and the end of the Cold War. Nepal's geo-political location and the strength of external pressures, direct or indirect, exerted either by colonial or by major post-colonial powers, have been determining factors in this formally independent state. Nevertheless, it is the internal play of forces, operating within the wider geo-political dynamic, that may yet play a crucial role in deciding the character of Nepal's governing institutions and overall political trajectory.[3]

Land, people, economy

Nepal is a roughly rectangular slab of 147,000 sq km, bordered on three sides by India along a perimeter of 1,746 km, and along its mountainous northern length of 1,100 km by the more inaccessible Tibetan plateau. Its population—around 28 million, comparable to that of Afghanistan—is overwhelmingly rural: barely 15 per cent of Nepalis are town-dwellers, and around 75 per cent earn their living through subsistence farming; equally, 75 per cent of fuel consumption is firewood. Geographically, the country comprises three ascending ecological belts. To the south, adjacent to India, is the fertile low-lying strip of the Tarai or plains region, home to 48 per cent of the population, mainly Madhesis. The central hill region—with altitudes ranging from around 600 to over 4,000 metres—including Kathmandu, has long dominated Nepali politics; it contains around 44 per cent of the population. Finally, there are the precipitous peaks of the north—Everest, etc—rising along the frontier with the People's Republic of China. The western hill and mountain regions have always been the poorest parts of the country and the strongest base of Communist support.

---

[3] In a historical perspective Nepal belongs to a category of third world countries—Thailand, Afghanistan, Ethiopia and even Iran—that were never colonized, had monarchical feudal-type rule but faced immense pressures, external and internal, in the course of the 20th century to carry out capitalist modernization. This would create potentially explosive socio-political tensions between the royal house and other rising elites as well as between dominant and exploited classes. But despite this common structural feature the actual trajectories, economic and political, taken by these countries have diverged sharply, leaving little ground for any fruitful comparative study. Thailand has undergone substantial capitalist development and retains a powerful constitutional monarchy in a semi-democracy. The greatest urban mass movement and insurrection of the last century swept away the monarchy in Iran only to replace it with an enduring and authoritarian clerical regime, overseeing capitalist expansion pivoted on indigenous oil and gas wealth. Ethiopia and Afghanistan experienced anti-Western urban-based revolutionary coups by radicalized sections of the military which sought to put in place policies of a 'socialist orientation', including radical land reform. But these never took off and today the two countries are ruled by pro-US authoritarian regimes. Nepal alone has experienced a classical peasant-based revolutionary upsurge that has overthrown monarchical rule, and carries a stronger promise of institutionalizing a more thoroughgoing democratic political system.

Nepal's ruling class has historically been drawn from the Newars, the indigenous elite of the hill region (5 per cent of the population, mainly based in Kathmandu) and from upper-caste Bahuns (Brahmins) and Chettris (Kshyatriyas), populations produced by the immigration to the region of Hindus from the south many centuries ago. Nepali, and its Devnagari script, spoken today by just over half the population, was derived from their Indo-Aryan languages. The indigenous peoples—now starting to define themselves as of 'pre-Aryan, Mongoloid stock'—live mostly in the hills but also in the Tarai, and speak Tibeto-Burman languages. Originally they followed Buddhist, Shamanist or Animist beliefs and practices, but today some of these groups have accepted a Hindu self-description, so that roughly 80 per cent of the population are now considered Hindu. These indigenous groups, known as Janajatis, now make up around 37 per cent of the total population; they were placed in the 'middle' of the caste system, below the Bahuns (12 per cent) and Chettris (19 per cent), and above the Dalits ('untouchables').[4] After the 1999 elections, the literate Bahun/Chettri/Newar category occupied 75 per cent of all cabinet posts and 61 per cent of all parliamentary seats. There was virtually no representation for Dalits (13 per cent) or Muslims (4 per cent). The Bahun/Chettri/Newar also hold 90 per cent of all positions in the civil services.[5]

In the Tarai region live the Madhesis or plains people of Indian origin, many of whom retain close ties with relatives across the border. Since landholdings here are larger, and feudal-type relations stronger, there are serious class contradictions among Madhesis, but these tend to be subsumed by the common cultural and social discriminations that all Madhesis face at the hands of hill peoples, whether B/C/N or Janajatis. They are often not seen as 'true' Nepalis and are subject to discrimination in employment by the state apparatus. Since 1990, there has been an explosion of groups taking up the Madhesi cause, as well as the rise

---

[4] In 2002, the government listed the existence of a total of 37 languages, and classified 59 Janajati groups for whom there would be reserved positions in education and administration.
[5] While the Chettris and scions of the Rana dynasty have dominated the upper echelons of the Royal Nepal Army, Dalits and Madhesis are effectively excluded, and members of the ethnic hill groups mostly make up the middle and lower ranks. The Gurkha regiments of Britain and India have come mainly from five such groups—the Magars (also a key support base for the Maoists), the Gurungs, the Limbus, the Tamangs and the Rais. Compared to their ambivalent status at home Gurkhas receive a more unequivocal respect and admiration abroad that reinforces their sense of loyalty to foreign employers.

of independent groups and older parties seeking to cash in on the griev-ances of Janajatis, Dalits and women.

One third of the Tarai population are immigrant hill peoples. Over 60 per cent of Dalits live in the hills, disproportionately more in the Mid- and Far West than in the East; the rest are in the Tarai. They remain basically landless and dependent on work in upper-caste owned larger terraced farms. In the West there is a larger proportion of Mongoloid ethnic groups who have subsistence plots than in the Eastern hills; many of these cannot ensure their families' livelihoods, hence their migration in substantial numbers to the Tarai and elsewhere. Their socio-cultural traditions make them more independent-minded, so feudal-type rela-tions of personal servility are weaker.

Landholding patterns remain unequal: the richest 5 per cent of house-holds own nearly 37 per cent of land, while some 47 per cent of landowning households own around 15 per cent of land, with an average size of 0.5 hectares. Though the average landholding of small farmers is slightly higher in the Western hills (0.52 hectares) than in the Eastern (0.47 hectares), the East is more agriculturally developed, with superior access to credit and investment, irrigation, fertilizers, technology, and so on. There has also historically been a significant regional difference in the degree of central government control, always weaker in the upper West than in the upper East; the early Nepali Communism of the 1950s first took root in the Western hills, a history of continuous left activism which benefited the Maoists later on. Of course, the CPN-M understood the necessity of expanding into the Central and Eastern regions so as to preclude any possibility of the Royal Nepal Army merely concentrating its military assaults on these Western strongholds. In more recent years, the Maoists have extended their social base from the rural poor to include lower level government servants, industrial labourers, small-scale busi-nessmen, teachers, students and unemployed graduates. There are some 100,000 rural youth who fail their high school board exams every year, while a significant portion of the 500,000 youth thrown yearly onto the job market do not get the jobs they feel qualified for.

According to the latest statistics available (2003–04), 31 per cent of Nepalis are below the poverty line, but this figure rises to 46 per cent of Dalits and 44 per cent of hill Janajatis, while geographically the figure is 45 per cent in the Mid-Western region and 41 per cent in the Far-Western region. If the international comparative measure of $2 a day (purchasing power parity) is used, then 66 per cent of Nepalis are poor. Whatever industry exists is largely in the Tarai, with few backward linkages. The informal sector (urban and rural) accounts for 90 per cent of all employment. In the countryside 16 per cent are totally landless while 63 per cent of the agricultural workforce are self-employed on the little land they have, or else engaged in rural work for others. These are the rural poor.

A post-colonial monarchy

The kingdom of Nepal was forged in the late 18th century by Prithvi Narayan Shah, ruler of the Gorkha principality (in present-day West Nepal), who captured Kathmandu in 1768 and absorbed the neighbouring rival states; today's royal family are his descendants. Originally stretching from Kashmir to Bhutan, Nepal was reduced to roughly its current size by the Sugouli peace agreement, following defeat by the forces of the British East India Company in the wars of 1814–16. In 1846, the pro-British Jang Bahadur carried out a Palace massacre and established a hereditary Rana premiership, in which successive members of the Rana dynasty ruled for personal wealth and power in the name of the titular king. The British, henceforth supplied with suicidally loyal Gurkha troops for their imperial wars, were happy to condone the Ranas' policy of isolating Nepal politically and economically from the outside world.

It was only after Indian Independence that Rana rule was finally overthrown, with Delhi's backing. A unified Nepal Congress party was formed in exile and, with King Tribhuvan's support, waged an armed struggle against the Rana government. In November 1950 the royal family took refuge in the Indian Embassy in Kathmandu, and were subsequently flown to Delhi. On 7 February 1951, caught between Indian pressure and armed opposition at home, the government agreed to the 'Delhi compromise', by which the King's powers were restored, and the Congress party and the Ranas formed a joint interim government, to establish a Constituent Assembly that would draw up a democratic constitution—a promise that has not been fulfilled to this day.[6] The 1854 Muluki Ain or 'country code' remained in force, establishing a single legal system but institutionalizing differential caste and sub-caste privileges and obligations, which persisted even after the government formally abolished

---

[6] As a measure of how strong Indian influence was at that time, New Delhi effectively set up the Royal Nepali Army and Nepal's civil services.

caste discrimination in 1963. The inequities associated with ethnic diversity and caste cleavages, far from being recognized and redressed, were ignored and subsumed in the name of a Nepali nationalism whose father-figure was the King and whose 'cultural unity' was expressed in the partisan symbols associated with the practices and values of upper-caste hill society.

Both Tribhuvan (1911–55) and his son Mahendra (1955–72) consolidated royal authority, assuming powers to appoint and dismiss the prime minister and cabinet. When a constitution was finally promulgated in 1959—a week before general elections—it vested maximum powers in the King. The Nepal Congress won a two-thirds majority under a first-past-the-post system and sought to implement a mild programme of state-led redistribution, including limited measures of land reform. This was enough to alarm the landed elites. On 15 December 1960, King Mahendra used his emergency powers to dissolve Parliament, arrest the Prime Minister, B. P. Koirala (elder brother of the current octogenarian Prime Minister G. P. Koirala) and ban all political parties, thereby laying the foundations for three decades of 'party-less' rule, sustained after Mahendra's death by his son King Birendra (1972–2001). The system, known as Panchayati Raj, involved a three-tier system of village, district and zonal assemblies—*panchayats*—which indirectly elected a national assembly with only advisory capacity to the King. Representative bodies for the five 'classes' of peasantry, women, youth, workers and ex-servicemen were permitted to exist under supervision, while there was also a firm separation between 'public' bodies controlled and monitored by the Palace and 'private' bodies such as newspapers, clubs, societies, professional associations, etc., which were excluded from political activity and subject to censorship and scrutiny. All this was sanctified by a new 1962 constitution, later somewhat amended after a mass student upsurge in 1979 and a subsequent 1980 referendum—widely believed to have been rigged—on the Panchayati Raj, which returned a narrow majority in favour of the existing system.

For obvious geographical, historical and cultural reasons, India has always been by far the most important political influence on Nepal; but any *pro forma* Indian objections to the consolidation of royal dictatorship in Nepal were modified by the Sino-Indian conflict in 1962, which also made it easier for New Delhi to accept CIA-supported bases of Tibetan Khampa rebels in two Nepali districts. For its part, Beijing's perspectives were clear: Nepal lies in India's 'sphere of influence' and this will not be challenged; but nor should Nepal become a haven for Tibetan dissidents or a base for interfering with China's control of the plateau. After the 1972 Sino-US entente these camps were closed, and Nepal–China political relations resumed on an even keel. Both Mahendra and Birendra sought to balance Indian influence through improved relations with China, and even in Mao's heyday Beijing was always more concerned to stabilize relations with the Palace in Kathmandu than to support popular struggles against it.[7]

Oppositions

Slowly, however, processes of modernization began to make inroads. The spread of educational and health facilities—if all too often of poor quality—helped raise the literacy level from 2 per cent in 1951 to 40 per cent in 1990. A professional middle class emerged in the towns and cities, demanding more socio-political space, while caste rituals and injunctions also weakened. The arrival of radio and the entry of foreign-aid missions helped put an end to the country's seclusion and created growing awareness of Nepal's comparative underdevelopment and lack of democracy, while expansion of the road network promoted internal and external migration. At the same time, the Palace project of heavy-handed unification and modernization from above could not but exacerbate social tensions. Banned parties went underground and continued their activities both within and outside the Panchayati system.

---

[7] Nor has the existence of Nepali Maoism hampered state-to-state relations or trade with China, not even including occasional arms purchases to be used against the Maoists. As recent as September 2005 there were reports of China having supplied $22 million of arms and ammunition and in November 2005, 18 trucks carrying military hardware were reported crossing the Nepal–Tibet border. This is not surprising. Nepali Maoism arose when Mao was in decline in China, and Nepali Maoists have never had serious organizational links with 'fraternal' parties outside, even in India. The CPN-M has helped set up a Coordinating Committee of Maoist Parties and Organizations of South Asia (CCOMPOSA) which has allowed some ideological interchange to take place, but even this body is largely inactive. Indian talk about a 'red corridor' of Maoism running from Nepal through central India down to the southern states is self-serving misinformation designed to exaggerate the 'Maoist threat' and justify repressive measures by New Delhi and state capitals, while diverting attention from development failures. The state governments also hope to attract greater financial largesse from the centre in the name of combating 'Naxalite terrorism'. Indian Maoism has expanded but is nothing like as widely and strongly rooted as is made out.

Nepali Communism, whose most distinctive characteristic has been its combination of endurance and fragmentation—in the late 1980s there were fifteen Communist parties, now reduced to half-a-dozen—provided a common if not a unified focus for agitation and growth.

The original Communist Party of Nepal was founded in 1949 under the leadership of Pushpa Lal Shrestha, and had strongly denounced the 1951 'Delhi compromise', seeing the Nepal Congress as a stooge of India and the King. In 1956, however, the CPN switched tack and recognized the King as constitutional head of state. Initially outlawed, the Party was now legalized, but has been bedevilled ever since both by personality clashes and ideological differences over the issue of reform versus revolution. The Sino-Soviet split had a greater and more lasting effect in Nepal than in India, where the 1964 break between the Communist Party of India and the Communist Party of India (Marxist) had more to do with differing orientations towards the Indian National Congress.

Broadly speaking, one could describe three basic trends within Nepali Communism. The first was a pro-Moscow Stalinism that over time mutated into a form of social democracy—though retaining a Communist label—with its primary ambition the establishment and stabilization of a parliamentary system in which it could pursue a more or less 'safe' reformist politics. By 1989, its principal legatee was the CPN-Marxist, which was soon to lose its rural poor base in its original strongholds of the upper Western region to the Maoists, even as it sought to secure support from rural and urban middle classes elsewhere. The initially more leftist pro-Beijing grouping split in two: one section later drifted towards social democracy and parliamentary reformism, mainly organized in the CPN-Marxist-Leninist, while the other remained true to its radical-Maoist origins. In the early 1970s, the Maoist upsurge in the Naxalbari region of West Bengal inspired a Nepali version of armed peasant rebellion against big landlords in the hilly Jhapa district of Eastern Nepal. Though eventually subdued, this is seen as the founding moment of Nepali Maoism, after which there would always remain a current of fluctuating strength committed to guerrilla struggle and the creation of rural 'base areas'. This third current was largely consolidated by 1989 as the CPN-Unity Centre, under the leadership of Pushpa Kamal Dahal, later better known as 'Prachanda'. A history of Nepali Communism would have to trace these three trajectories and their inter-relations, replete with the fission and fusion of groups, parties and fronts, and including political-ideological crossovers.

First Jan Andolan

Against this backdrop, various other developments paved the way for the mass upsurge known as the Jan Andolan of February 1990, which would lead to the collapse of the dictatorial Panchayati Raj. An important factor was the hardship caused by the Indian trade blockade imposed by Rajiv Gandhi's Congress government—as a rebuke for Kathmandu's import of Chinese arms and failure to clamp down on cross-border smuggling— when the 1950 Trade and Transit Treaty, vital for landlocked Nepal, came up for renewal in 1989. If the decision to squeeze Nepal through prolonged blockade initially created widespread resentment against India, the public mood soon changed to one of increasing anger, not just at the Palace's failure to resolve matters with New Delhi but against the whole monarchical system. At the same time, the broader struggles for democracy in the second half of the 1980s—the successful overthrow of the Marcos regime in the Philippines in 1986, the emergence of glasnost and perestroika, Tiananmen, the East European movements of 1989— had a very substantial resonance in Nepal, especially among the urban intellectuals and activists who were key drivers of the upsurge.

Internally, the most important development began with the establishment of a working unity between the two biggest left parties, the formerly pro-Moscow CPN-Marxist and the formerly pro-Beijing CPN-ML.[8] Along with some smaller groups, these formed a United Left Front which in turn, through the autumn and winter of 1989, forged an alliance with the Nepal Congress and announced the launching of a Movement for the Restoration of Democracy, to begin on 18 February 1990, the anniversary of the 1951 overthrow of Rana rule.[9] What the leaders of the MRD never anticipated was the remarkable response they received from the

---

[8] The CPN-ML's initial stronghold was in the Eastern hills among small and middle peasantry—the Jhapa legacy. This base was transferred to the merger of the two parties, the CPN-Unified Marxist-Leninist. The CPN-UML subsequently shifted towards representing the interests of the middle class and petit-bourgeois of town and country, and then those of the higher professionals and sections of the upper classes. The social base of the CPN-UML overlaps with that of the Nepali Congress and CPN-Maoist, more so with the latter.

[9] This pattern of prior collaboration between left and right to promote an antimonarchical democratic mass movement was to repeat itself in the run-up to the 'second democratic revolution' of April 2006.

public, with widespread mass demonstrations and strikes by students, teachers, government employees, workers and medics. In the course of this movement, to the dismay of the Palace, the V. P. Singh government in India as well as London and Washington gave formal support to the MRD, though China remained warily aloof.

The turning point came on 6 April 1990, when half a million people came out on the streets in a victory celebration, after King Birendra had announced the formation of a new cabinet that would begin negotiations with the MRD leaders. When a section of the crowd in Kathmandu began marching toward the Palace, the Army opened fire, following this with shooting elsewhere as other demonstrations broke out with new force. No accurate account of the death toll has emerged. But this bloodbath created such public horror and anger that the King effectively capitulated, to save his status as a father-figure of the nation. By 13 April the ban on parties had been lifted and political prisoners released, a new interim cabinet was installed with Congress and Communist members, and the basic institutions of Panchayati Raj were completely dissolved.

In November 1990 a new constitution was finally promulgated, reducing the powers of the King but still retaining provisions that ensured that the changes would remain partial and unsatisfactory. Above all, the three cornerstones of the old regime—monarchy, Nepali language dominance, Hinduism—remained intact. The King was still Commander-in-Chief of the Royal Nepal Army and retained wide-reaching emergency powers. The multi-ethnic and multi-lingual character of Nepal was recognized but Nepali remained the only state language, and Hinduism the state religion. That this was too limited an outcome soon became evident, since the MRD had unleashed a powerful new dynamic of lower-caste and ethnic mobilizations that would have to be addressed if a unified and truly democratic state was eventually to emerge. It would take another sixteen years for an even wider and deeper mass movement to arise, aiming to complete the project of a democratic restructuring of the Nepali state, and this time demand not, as in 1990, the constitutionalization of the monarchy, but its complete abolition.

The period from 1990 to 2002 has been described as 'anarchic democracy'.[10] For the first time political parties were allowed to function, and

---

[10] The term is that of Kanak Mani Dixit, editor of *Himal*, perhaps the most widely known internationally of Nepal's political journals.

civil-society groups and leaders emerged; ethnic and caste conscious-ness escalated, along with a determination to eradicate discrimination. Income disparities were also growing: between 1995 and 2004, the Gini coefficient rose from 34.2 to 41.4, with larger gaps opening up between the rich and the middle-income layers, as well as between the middle and the poor. Migration—above all to India, but also to East and South-East Asia and the Arab countries—increased dramatically: the real total of remittances, official and unofficial, was estimated at some 25 per cent of GDP. While domestic development continued to stagnate, Nepal was becoming a remittance economy par excellence.[11]

The 1991 national assembly elections, the first since 1959, were won by the Nepal Congress with 38 per cent of the votes and 110 seats, out of 205. More surprising were the 69 seats won (with 28 per cent of the vote—the first-past-the-post disparities speak for themselves) by the newly united Communist Party, the CPN-Unified Marxist-Leninist. In the 1994 elections, the CPN-UML won 88 seats to the Nepal Congress's 83 and formed the first-ever Communist-led national government in South Asia—although it was brought down within a year as coalition alliances shifted in favour of the Nepal Congress. The CPN-UML itself then split, with both factions now competing to enter governing coali-tions with the Nepal Congress. All in all, the period from 1990 to 2002 saw thirteen changes of government, accompanied by unscrupulous displays of power-brokering and self-centred party manoeuvres, with no real attempts to address the immense problems facing the country; it is hardly surprising that the appeal of the radical left should have grown.

The Maoists of the CPN-Unity Centre, meanwhile, had used the platform of the 1991 elections to expose the inability of parliamentary politics to

---

[11] India is said to have 65 per cent of all Nepali migrants, with a further 18 per cent in Arab countries, about 2 per cent in the UK, and the rest in Malaysia, Bhutan, China, South Korea, Hong Kong, Japan and the US. There are no accurate figures for how many Nepali migrants there are in India, as against Indians of Nepali ori-gin, which migrants may in due course become; estimates vary between 2 million and 6 million. Officially, remittances in 2003–04 came to approximately $800 mil-lion or 12 per cent of Nepal's GDP. However, if illegal inward flows and Indian currency simply brought over the border are added—Indian rupees are legal tender and accepted everywhere—the real total of remittances would be more than dou-ble that. Officially, in 2003–04, 35 per cent of this came from Qatar, Saudi Arabia and UAE, compared with 30 per cent from India. *Resilience Amidst Conflict: An Assessment of Poverty in Nepal: 1995/96 and 2003/04*, prepared by the World Bank, June 2006, pp. 51–8.

resolve the basic problems of land reform, Dalit and gender discrimination and oppressed nationalities; they called for a new 'democratic revolution', based on the dictatorship of the proletariat and peasantry, to do this. They won 9 seats (on 4 per cent of the vote), thus emerging as the third party in Parliament. But the group—which would change its name to CPN-Maoist in 1995—was already making political and organizational preparations, internally and externally, for a turn towards protracted people's war, formally announced on 13 February 1996. The armed struggle started in the traditional Communist/Maoist strongholds of the Mid- and Far-West. The CPN-M began by attacking local banks, burning loan papers to indebted farmers, stealing money, attacking police stations, accumulating small arms and making cross-border black market purchases of more sophisticated weaponry; later, they would assault Royal Nepal Army district headquarters and acquire machine guns and rocket-launchers. By 2000, they were emerging as a force at national level.

Initially, neither King Birendra nor the Parliamentary leadership had taken the CPN-M's declaration of armed struggle too seriously, thinking police action would be enough to crush such adventurism. From 2000 onwards, however, both India and the US urged the more cautious King to send the RNA to confront the Maoists directly. Finally in April 2001 Birendra dispatched his troops against the Maoist villages, in the (most un-Nepali) name of an 'Integrated Security and Development Programme'.

Murder at the palace

Two months later, on 1 June 2001, came the extraordinary royal blood-bath at the Palace in Kathmandu, when the 'crazed' Crown Prince Dipendra allegedly murdered his father, King Birendra, along with his mother the Queen, and his royal sister and brother, before shooting himself in the head. Birendra's brother, Gyanendra, was duly crowned King of Nepal on June 4th. The circumstances surrounding this episode were sufficiently murky for the overwhelming majority of the Nepali people to believe, rightly or wrongly, that the whole thing had been a conspiracy hatched by Gyanendra. The new King lost little time in displaying his ruthless authoritarian character, or political ineptitude: within six months of his coronation his Congress Prime Minister, Bahadur Deuba, had been instructed to impose emergency rule, citing among other things the Maoist threat.

Washington and Delhi fully supported King Gyanendra's November 2001 declaration of emergency—adding substance to the view that they had also been party to a conspiracy against Birendra. From then until Gyanendra's February 2005 Palace coup, both capitals gave sustained political-military support to his efforts to crush the Maoists. India provided some $90 million worth of arms; the top echelons of the Royal Nepal Army have always had close relations with their counterparts in the Indian army and its main intelligence agency, known as the Research and Analysis Wing. For its part, the US consolidated relations with the RNA in the 2001–04 period, when Christina Rocca was Assistant Secretary of State for South Asia. In mid-2001 an 'Office of Defense Cooperation' was set up at the US Embassy in Kathmandu, US military advisers arrived to help plot the defeat of the Maoists and a programme of sending RNA officers to US army colleges and training centres was established. In this period Washington collaborated with the BJP-led Delhi government, which assented to such co-ordination despite India's long-standing policy of seeking to monopolize external influence over the RNA. In January 2002 Colin Powell became the highest-ranking American government official ever to visit Nepal, and afterwards $12 million of a promised $20 million was released for arms purchases. In the course of the civil war that followed, the Royal Nepal Army quadrupled in size, to over 90,000 troops, and spread to areas of the country where it had never ventured before.

Waging people's war

Despite this onslaught, by the beginning of 2005 the Maoists had spread to all but two of the country's seventy-five districts, and claimed to control 80 per cent of the countryside. During this period the CPN-M sustained a highly organized underground political structure, topped by a Standing Committee of seven members, below which was a Politbureau of fifteen, then a Central Committee of forty to fifty, which oversaw five regional bureaux of the East, Centre, West, Kathmandu and Abroad (mainly India-based supporters). The first three regional bureaux each supervised three sub-regions, and there were district committees at the base.[12] In the regions they controlled, the Maoists set up base areas and people's committees at the levels of ward, village, district and sub-region, and carried out local development work and social programmes

---

[12] Since the CPN-M emerged from underground, the top two rungs have been replaced by an eleven-member Central Secretariat, with the former Central Committee reduced to thirty-five members and renamed the Central Organizing Committee.

of inter-caste marriage, widow remarriage and temperance campaigns, with varying degrees of effectiveness. From 2003 the Maoists moved into the Tarai border regions, where they spread like wildfire, since they more than any other political force had long articulated the demand for equality of 'nationalities' such as the Madhesis. But the very speed with which they widened their appeal, even as it emboldened and assured them in a strategic sense, also blinded them to the underlying reality. A powerful new Madhesi dynamic had been unleashed, which in due course would escape the Maoists' control and benefit other forces with much deeper historical roots that had stronger class, caste and patronage structures working for them, once they too began taking up Madhesi grievances and demands.

Throughout the whole period of armed struggle there was also legal work through various front organizations of workers, peasants, 'nationalities', oppressed castes, students, intellectuals and women, expressing the Maoists' demands and their overall political vision. Amid all the talk of having proceeded steadily through the successive phases of strategic defence and strategic balance to finally reach the phase of strategic offensive, it is notable that the Maoists never tried to hold on to the district capitals they attacked. Accurate estimates of Maoist armed strength are hard to come by. One source says that by 2005 the Maoists had a highly motivated force of 10,000 trained and armed guerrillas—the People's Liberation Army divided into some nine brigades, in turn subdivided into battalions, companies and platoons—plus a further 20,000 armed militia divided into a secondary force of mobile squads and more stationary base forces.[13]

Strategically, the CPN-M was perhaps most strongly influenced—apart from by Mao's own classic perspective—by the Sendero Luminoso's near success in Peru, seeing its final failure as reflecting a 'left deviationism', just as it sees the Sandinista defeat of the late eighties after achieving power as the failure of a 'right deviationism'. Its ideological vision of the path to socialism has been shaped by a positive interpretation of the Great Proletarian Cultural Revolution, which despite its excesses is perceived as a crucial attempt to prevent bureaucratic degeneration through a 'mass line' approach, hence the enduring admiration for Mao himself. It has also been affected by the subsequent experiences of the

---

[13] International Crisis Group, 'Nepal's Maoists: Their Aims, Structure and Strategy', 27 October 2005.

former Communist world, to the point where Nepal's Maoists have formally and publicly adopted a position in favour of genuine multi-party competition even in the 'socialist phase', as well as accepting the existence of independent trade unions and their right to strike. On the current experiences of the Latin American left, in Venezuela and Bolivia, the leadership's position is that these are on the whole positive, but it needs to know more. Hesitant to advise their Indian comrades, the farthest that Prachanda and Bhattarai—the top two leaders—will go is to say that in the more industrially developed India, much more attention has to be paid to organizing in the cities and open mass work.[14]

Royal coup

Even as Maoist influence grew, King Gyanendra continued to concentrate power in his own hands. In May 2002 he dissolved Parliament; he dismissed the Deuba ministry five months later and replaced it with his own appointees. Finally, in February 2005, a parade of unelected governments was ended when the King sacked the Prime Minister and Cabinet, vested their executive powers in himself, arrested the country's political leaders and suspended civil liberties. Gyanendra succeeded in making himself the most hated king in Nepal's history. If a substantial majority of the population now want a republic, this is because a weaker but more general dissatisfaction with the monarchical system has fused with a real contempt for Gyanendra to create a deep hostility to the institution itself. So strong is the current revulsion that even the Nepal Congress, a key repository of varied royalist convictions, publicly declared its commitment to republicanism on 6 September 2007.

The CPN-M itself came close to a split in 2004–05, with differences over strategic issues exacerbated by an emerging personality cult around Prachanda. The rift focused around the balance between political and military action, which in turn related to a long-standing divergence within the party as to whether the struggle against the Nepali monarchy should take priority, or whether it should be subordinated to the needs of a national-popular defence against 'Indian expansionism'; a strong current within the CPN-M had long seen King Birendra as a Sihanouk-like 'royal nationalist' and potential ally against the great power to the south. The

---

[14] Personal conversations in October 2007 with Prachanda and Baburam Bhattarai. Prachanda comes from a poor peasant background and Bhattarai from a middle peasant background. Both were radicalized as students in the late sixties or early seventies.

debate was finally settled in favour of the anti-monarchist position, itself powerfully vindicated when Gyanendra turned against the mainstream parties in February 2005. The latter's struggle for survival effectively pushed them towards the Maoists, who were quick to grasp the exceptionally favourable shift in the domestic and international relationship of forces that had taken place, as the King continued to isolate himself both domestically and internationally. By mid-2005 the Indian government was becoming conscious of the changing internal situation in Nepal, and the futility of continuing its support for Gyanendra. It now changed tack and sought to 'tame' the CPN-M, by bringing them into a stabilized electoral and parliamentary process, while retaining its longer-term perspective of working to finally eliminate the Maoist threat. The US, much slower to understand the changes, opposed the November 2005 Memorandum of Understanding, partly brokered by India, between the Maoists and the mainstream parties, and continued to keep the Maoists on its terrorist list; but even Washington eventually decided to oppose Gyanendra's blatantly dictatorial turn. It would have been folly not to take advantage of such conditions.

In discussions with the author in October 2007, Prachanda gave two reasons for not seeking to seize state power militarily in 2005, when it seemed within their grasp, but instead turning to negotiate a permanent peace settlement, involving a long-term strategic alliance with the mainstream parties to fight for a 'democratic republic'. First, given the international balance of forces, the Maoist leadership believed that, while they might capture state power, they would not be able to retain it. Second, by abandoning the path of armed struggle for peaceful mass mobilization they hoped to achieve a new legitimacy, domestically and internationally, that would afford them greater protection in the long run. This turn was one that many of the CPN-M's own cadres, educated in the belief that they were fighting for a thoroughgoing people's democracy, found hard to swallow. The new line that was finally accepted was that the democratic republic, though seemingly bourgeois in form, was actually a transitional phase towards a future people's democracy, and that progress along this 'peaceful' path would be gauged by the extent to which the key tasks of overcoming class oppression (above all, the question of land reform), eliminating caste and gender oppression, and resolving the 'nationalities' question (federal restructuring of the state) were actually carried out.

However, this strategic shift was almost certainly influenced by the awareness that to try and achieve a climactic military victory against a force of 15,000 to 20,000 stationed to protect Kathmandu would be bloody and uncertain. As it was, some 13,000 had died in the civil war, of which 7,000 to 8,000 were probably civilian third parties. If most of these deaths were caused by the Royal Nepal Army, the Maoists were far from blameless.

Second Jan Andolan

Urban opposition to Gyanendra's February 2005 coup was first organized by trade union groups, progressive NGOs, and teachers' and lawyers' associations. An umbrella organization, the Citizens' Movement for Democracy and Peace, brought together some of the country's leading public intellectuals,[15] and pushed the mainstream parties to unite in the campaign for democracy. In mid 2005, the Seven-Party Alliance (SPA) was formed.[16] On 22 November 2005, with Indian government backing, the SPA and the Maoists concluded a twelve-point Memorandum of Understanding: both sides would unite to end monarchical autocracy, restore Parliament, establish an all-party interim government, call for a Constituent Assembly, acknowledge past mistakes and allow each other freedom of political activity everywhere; and—with the help of 'appropriate international supervision'—work to end the conflict between the Royal Nepal Army and the PLA.

In March 2006, the SPA and the Maoists agreed to launch a joint Jan Andolan II on 6 April, commemorating the climax of the 1990 Jan Andolan I. For tactical reasons, and to obviate fears of a Maoist takeover, the CPN-M encouraged the SPA to lead the mass mobilizations in Kathmandu and the other cities, while they provided large-scale logistical support and brought in huge numbers of their own supporters.

---

[15] These included Devinder Raj Pandey, a former cabinet minister and leader of the civil society movement; Krishna Khanal and Mahesh Maskey, professors at Kathmandu's Tribhuvan University; Shyam Shrestha, respected journalist and his wife Mukta Shrestha, well-known social worker; Khagendra Sangraula, poet and literary critic; and Shanta Shrestha, a famous human-rights activist campaigning since the 1950s.

[16] These were the Nepal Congress, the breakaway Nepal Congress (Democratic), the CPN-UML, the left-wing Janamorcha Nepal (People's Movement Nepal), the Tarai-based Nepal Sadbhavna Party, the Nepal Workers' and Peasants' Party, and the United Left Front. On 25 September 2007 the NC and NC(D) merged, making it now a six-party alliance.

The former Nepal Congress prime minister, G. P. Koirala—the crafty and experienced 'grand old man' of Nepali politics, with no love for the Maoists—was nonetheless seen as one of the key leaders of a movement created mainly, but not only, by this inter-party collaboration.[17] There was widespread and spontaneous involvement of popular groups, which increasingly began to include the middle classes, and finally even the cadres of such key state institutions as the Reserve Bank of Nepal.

The remarkable 19-day upsurge of Jan Andolan II, which at its height on 23 and 24 April 2006 brought over a million people into the streets, pushed well beyond the goals envisaged by New Delhi. Despite differences between the Congress and non-Congress prime ministers in India—I. K. Gujral, V. P. Singh, Chandra Shekhar—both sides have usually operated a 'two-pillar' approach with regard to Nepal, working both through the Nepal Congress and the Palace. This had allowed India to shift its emphasis from the Palace to the parliamentary system and back again as circumstances were deemed to dictate: to appear as both pro-monarchy and pro-democracy. Such meddling backfired badly when, at the height of the 2006 Jan Andolan agitation, New Delhi sent a scion of the former royal family of Kashmir, Karan Singh, to King Gyanendra, in the hope of getting him to offer some compromise formula and thus save one 'pillar', the monarchy. On 21 April Gyanendra duly invited the SPA to name a new prime minister, an offer roundly rejected by the Alliance which declared that it would organize a two-million-strong march on the Palace on 27 April.

On the 24th, the king capitulated. He conceded all the main demands of the twelve-point Memorandum of Understanding, agreeing to shed all executive powers and restore Parliament. The SPA and the public hailed this as a great victory, while the Maoists, concerned that this might be the end of the process rather than just the beginning, expressed their concerns at a possible 'betrayal'. However, such was the public mood and pressure that in May 2006 Parliament was restored, Koirala became Prime Minister of an interim SPA government, Nepal was formally declared a secular state, the RNA was brought under civilian control and

---

[17] Despite Koirala's well-deserved reputation for being pro-India and for unscrupulous trickery, he had burnished his credentials through his unwavering opposition to Gyanendra since 2002, and as Nepal Congress president had expelled Prime Minister Deuba from the party after the latter had dissolved Parliament at the King's behest in May 2002.

renamed the Nepal Army, and negotiations were opened between the government and the Maoists.

Dilemmas of transition

The heady optimism of the Maoists in the immediate aftermath of Jan Andolan II soon gave way to a sense of alarm. As noted above, the preponderance of first-past-the-post, constituency-based voting in the planned Constituent Assembly elections, to which the Maoists had at first consented, was liable to leave them with perhaps a sixth of the seats and scant influence in determining future policy outcomes. In the triangular power game played out since May 2006 between the Congress, the CPN-UML and the CPN-M, the latter two are programmatically closer but, for that very reason, also have substantially overlapping social bases. The Maoists worry that the CPN-UML will eat into their actual or potential electoral base, while the leaders of the CPN-UML are concerned that the radicalism of the Maoists will attract much of their cadre and that the Maoists, despite their current call for left unity, have a longer-term plan to split their party. During the drafting of the interim constitution, Prime Minister Koirala as the head of the SPA could make use of these tensions to outmanoeuvre the Maoists. Not only did the interim constitution, declared in mid-January 2007, enshrine a mixed, parallel voting system—the CPN-UML had to content itself with a dissenting note in favour of full proportional representation—but it made no specific reference to federalism, only committing itself to put an end to the unitary state. These two lapses seriously undermined Maoist influence among the indigenous groups, including the Madhesis of the Tarai.

At the news of the interim constitution's failure to enshrine a federal basis for a future Nepali state, a spontaneous and angry mass movement erupted among the Madhesis, in which all kinds of forces participated—ex-Maoist leaders who had formed their own groups; the Nepal Congress; and the Hindu right, backed by its Indian counterparts, who saw in this upsurge the chance to undermine popular support for the Maoists. Major landowning and politically powerful families in Uttar Pradesh and Bihar, often with criminal links, have long been intervening to substantial effect in the politics of the Tarai, while the Hindutva forces of India have seen the world's only Hindu kingdom as an expression of a Hindu *rashtra* which—unlike India itself—has not been tainted historically by Muslim or Christian invasion and rule.[18] In early 2007, forty people were killed by police gunfire during the 21-day mass uprising in the Tarai. The protests were led by an ex-Maoist, Upendra Yadav, who had formed the Madhesi Jan Adhikar Forum (Madhesi People's Rights Forum) as the main rival to the Maoists' own Madhesi Mukti Morcha (Madhesi Liberation Front).

If the Maoists were embittered by these 'pretenders' now usurping their agenda, they hardly helped matters by advocating a tough law-and-order line by the central government against these and subsequent Madhesi mobilizations. In the following months the Tarai was largely to escape Kathmandu's control. With a defunct administration, a political vacuum had opened that was filled by some twenty-two armed groups, many of them criminal. Armed clashes including the killing of activists took place between the Maoist organizations and other groups. Other sources of tension were between the state and the Madhesis, among Madhesi groups themselves, and between Madhesis and settlers of hill origin, especially as there also emerged extreme Madhesi groups demanding expulsion of these settlers from the Tarai and even independence from Nepal. In all this could be seen the hand of India, keen to promote hostility to the Maoists. After inordinate delay Kathmandu finally agreed in September 2007 to some key Madhesi demands: a commission of inquiry into the police shootings, compensation payments, and an assurance that it would be constitutionally sensitive to the Madhesis' desire for respect and equality. But there has been no forward movement on this score, and the Tarai continues to simmer. Indeed, a new Tarai party has been formed led by a few parliamentary defectors from the NC and CPN-UML, while violence escalated towards the close of 2007.

---

[18] The connection between Nepali and Indian politics takes place at a number of levels, although it is the Indian state that has always been the crucial factor. Hindutva forces have always had a link with the Palace, but the enduring weakness of the Hindu right in Nepali civil society—understandable given the country's diversity and its history of monarchical authoritarian rule—has always posed huge problems. The Hindu right has so far not been able to seriously shape Nepal's politics, although it can cause mischief. On 1 September 2004, after twelve Nepalis were abducted and killed in Iraq, the Nepali Hindu right engineered attacks on Muslims, the first time Kathmandu had witnessed such communal riots in which it is believed that the Palace silently acquiesced. No credible investigation was held nor were the culprits ever found.

Elsewhere, in Kathmandu and other towns, the revival of the Maoists' Young Communist League in late 2006 has proved to be double-edged. The idea was to provide an outlet for their radical cadre, including many of their ex-militia and PLA activist-leaders; to have an electoral mobilizing force, and an organization that would gather mass support through social work and progressive campaigns. Despite some success in unearthing public scandals, the YCL—some 200,000 strong and comprising Maoist cadre-members of all kinds, including newly recruited opportunist goons in towns and villages—has also succeeded in alienating large sections of the public through the still militarized mindsets of too many of their activists and leaders and, in places, resort to extortion, partly for electoral purposes. The CPN-M does not receive financial backing from business and wealthy elites in the way that the Congress and CPN-UML do. These two parties are also accused of illegally diverting international aid money, and it is widely believed that New Delhi also does its bit for them. However, this does not justify YCL high-handedness, and on 26 November 2007 in the *Kathmandu Post*, Prachanda had to give a public assurance that the YCL would change its behaviour and shed its negative image.

But if Maoist reservations, ruthlessness and ineptitude are one part of the explanation for the difficulties of the transition, the more important part resides with those still unwilling to give up the option of ultimately isolating and eliminating the Maoists. Here, the absolutely key issue is that of 'security sector reform'. Koirala, as we have seen, refused to take the action that was within his power in the aftermath of Jan Andolan II. Although the interim government carried out a shake-up of the police and paramilitary forces, the Prime Minister refused to make any changes within the upper echelons of the Army, claiming that any such move would 'destabilize' Nepal's political situation. Nor has he taken any steps to 'democratize' the armed forces or move towards an eventual merger of the Nepal Army and PLA, though long-term peace is only possible if an assured and honourable place is found for members of the latter. In fact, over the course of 2006 it became increasingly evident that he had done a deal with the Army top brass. They will assure Koirala and the Congress of their support in return for his leaving the existing military leadership in place, along with its freedom to make defence contracts, and deferring any merger with the PLA. In short, Koirala, Delhi and Washington have so far remained united in their determination to keep the army as their weapon of last resort against the Maoists.[19] As long as this is the case, the prospect of a permanent peace is being subordinated to the retention of the military option, even if this means another round of civil war.

A breakthrough in reform of the security sector might now have to follow a more general forward movement in the overall political situation. This means that the SPA–Maoist alliance, tension-filled though it is, needs to be sustained. A division at this time would make much more difficult a peaceful fulfilment of the key joint demands pertaining to a constitutionally sanctioned restructuring of the state. In this regard the special session of the Parliament on 4 November 2007 played an important role in creating positive momentum. The CPN-M and CPN-UML united to jointly pass by simple majority a resolution demanding a full PR voting system, while leaving open the issue of an immediate declaration of a republic. This resolution could not come into constitutional force without a two-thirds parliamentary majority, i.e., without Congress support. But Koirala was isolated and outmanoeuvred. Over the next one-and-a-half months, amidst warnings of starting a Jan Andolan III to fulfil the 'majority will' expressed in Parliament, a deal was finally struck between the 'big three' and the interim constitution amended by the requisite two-thirds Parliamentary vote at the end of December 2007. An immediate declaration abolished the monarchy; this act was to be ratified (without voting) by the future elected Constituent Assembly, which would now have a total of 601 seats, of which 240 would remain first-past-the-post constituencies, 335 seats would be decided by PR and the remaining 26 appointed (through consensus) by the Prime Minister; thus representing a roughly 56: 40 breakdown, well short of the 100 percent PR demanded. The Maoists also rejoined the interim government, reclaiming the five people-oriented Cabinet portfolios—physical planning and housing, local development, forestry, communications, women, children and social welfare—they had earlier given up, and gaining two junior ministerships. Security sector reform (as had long been promised) would now,

---

[19] Most Nepalis will support the recent extension of the UN Mission in Nepal to July 2008, to continue to monitor the peace process and oversee the CA elections if and when they take place. But both China and India feel uneasy about the prolonged presence of UNMIN, fearing this might set dangerous precedents for possible UN involvement in Kashmir and Tibet, where widespread human rights abuses certainly exist.

Koirala said, definitely be initiated even if only completed well after the Constituent Assembly elections, now scheduled for 10 April 2008.

What, then, have the Maoists got from this new compromise settlement? Undoubtedly their greatest gain is that they garner the fullest credit for establishing a republic. By pushing the Congress to accept this declaration before the elections they have greatly reduced, though not eliminated, the danger of a royalist army coup, as well as what is called the 'Bangladesh Option'—military rule behind a civilian façade (provided above all by the Congress), posing as a necessary 'stabilizer' and 'protector' in a situation of 'unacceptable' anarchy. Despite the small increase in PR the CPN-M will in all probability remain the third party after the elections. But there is now more chance of it being able to accumulate enough seats to be a 'balancer' between the Congress and CPN-UML, both in the Constituent Assembly and the future governmental coalition.

Is it possible that the rescheduled elections—already twice postponed— could again be derailed? Should this happen it would be an unmitigated disaster. The SPA–Maoist alliance would most probably break up. Royalist groups particularly, and anti-Maoist forces generally (including the Nepal Army), would get fresh impetus as the country plunges into deep uncertainty, with the resumption of civil war and greater anarchy in the Tarai becoming much more likely.

There are three possible sources for such a dangerous denouement. First, security sector reform must begin, or alternatively the Maoists be convinced that this process will become unstoppable after the Constituent Assembly elections. Second, current Madhesi turmoil has created a powder-keg situation in the Tarai. If Madhesi grievances are not seriously addressed, holding elections in the Tarai (and therefore nationally) may prove impossible by the scheduled date. Third, the 'big three' have repeatedly subordinated wider public interests to their particularist ambitions, as reflected in the various political manoeuvrings and shifting tactical alliances in which each has engaged. The public image of all three parties has consequently suffered. Besides widespread hope there is also a significant measure of disillusionment. It remains to be seen how these will play out when the most important elections in the history of Nepal are finally held.

1 February 2008

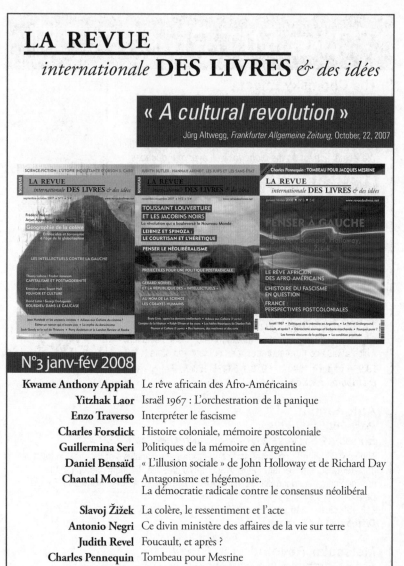

INTRODUCTION TO ROSSANA ROSSANDA

The history of European Communism has been written in many ways, by participants, opponents, students of the labour movement. Among memorialists, Rossana Rossanda cuts an unusual figure. Born in 1924, daughter of a prosperous notary from Istria ruined in the Great Depression, she entered university in Milan, still quite unpolitical, in 1941. Two years later, with German armies in control of North Italy, and Mussolini's Social Republic installed at Salò, she joined the Resistance, at the age of nineteen. A Communist in the underground, by 1947 she was working full-time in the PCI and rose through the Milan Federation to the Central Committee in 1960. By then she was an editor of the party's influential weekly Rinascita. *Togliatti, appreciating her gifts, put her in charge of the cultural department of the PCI in 1962, and she was elected a deputy in the Italian Parliament. When the student revolt exploded in 1967–68, however, she expressed sympathy for a movement viewed with suspicion by the PCI leadership, and helped to create the first periodical in the party's history critical of official positions from the left,* Il Manifesto. *Denounced at the Twelfth Party Congress, the* Manifesto *Group was expelled from the PCI in November 1969, going on to create the independent daily of the same name that continues to this day.*

For nearly four decades, Rossanda has been its most individual editorialist and commentator, writing with a cool, unrhetorical tranchant *that has made hers a unique signature in the Italian press. Characteristic of her interventions has been a consistent attention to the social, in a culture more typically riveted by the political, in its narrower senses. In 2005, her memoir of the first forty-five years of her life,* La Ragazza del Secolo Scorso, *extracts of which are translated below, was published to widespread literary acclaim. In it, reflecting on her role as a young woman with responsibility in the party, and the hesitations she felt in exercising it, she remarks, in a tone that gives something of the tenor of her memoir: 'Not that women do not love power, they exercise it without mercy in private and against each other. But outside private life, we are tempted to follow, however torn, paths decided by others. We feel extraneous to such decisions, and like Virginia Woolf make a point of this, not without tears and complaints at the upshot. But we rarely question that feeling, because that leads to less violence—and that might be a virtue—but also to less responsibility, which I doubt is one'.*

ROSSANA ROSSANDA

THE COMRADE FROM MILAN

THIS IS NOT a history.[1] It is simply what my memory supplies when I see the dubious looks of those around me: why were you a Communist? Why do you say that you still are? What do you mean? Is it an illusion that you are clinging to, through stubbornness, through ossification? Every so often someone will stop me and say 'You were my heroine!' But what does that mean? The cycle of Communism and the Communists in the 20th century finished so badly that it is impossible not to ask these questions. What did it mean to become a Communist in 1943? A Party member, not just a philosophical adherent whose position could be justified with an 'I had nothing to do with that'. I started asking them of myself and searching for the answers—without looking at books or documents; but not without doubts.

September 1939

At the time it did not feel like a rupture. Our family was in the Dolomites, my sister Mimma and I—she was twelve, I was fifteen—looked out for the first autumn colours in the meadows that would signal it was time to leave for Milan. The days went by as normal, while Poland was divided up between the Germans and the Russians; but Poland was far away, the Soviet Union even farther. There had always been a rumble of military news on the radio. The Spanish Civil War had brought us noisy propaganda about nuns and priests with their throats cut, planes taking off from Italy, bloodthirsty Communists, the siege of Alcázar, Teruel, Guadalajara, Madrid. Our family adopted its standard approach: silence and deafness. It was not a question of fear; nobody close to us had been beaten up by the Fascists, and the violence of the Mussolini regime had abated by the 1930s. Ours was a non-fascism, not an anti-fascism; a slightly scornful attempt to stay aloof.

Even when the war began to materialize into tangible things—diversions, shortages, rules—it still seemed to have the character of a natural disaster rather than a human one. I was at the Liceo Manzoni in Milan. I plunged into the works of philosophy my father brought home for me—Eucken, Windelband—lying face-down on the carpet. I was determined to go to University a year early, starting in the autumn of 1941. I had never felt so good in my skin as when I entered that beautiful courtyard in the Corso di Porta Romana. I read History of Art with Matteo Marangoni, Philosophy and Aesthetics with Antonio Banfi. These two teachers remade me: Marangoni taught me how to look at a painting or a statue, indicating with the long shadow of his pointer on the black-and-white slide projection: 'Look here, and here: how right it is.' Right—*giusto*—indicated something absolute. His work on Baroque Art has remained one of the great books; it spoke of a time of upheaval, of violence and its rationalization; confusedly, we felt the need to think about such times, that, as Marangoni let us know. Banfi opened the world of the Warburg Library's thinkers to us: Panofsky, Wölfflin, Cassirer. His approach was the opposite of determinist; he showed us the confusion of the past, the contradictory clashes and collisions that yielded a history that had neither ends nor end, woven between reality and possibility.

Spring 1943

Nobody talked about a 'lightning war' any more. Victory proclamations for the Pact of Steel barely masked the increasing indications of disaster. At first the Allied bombing seemed almost unreal. After the sirens had sounded my mother and I stood by the window watching the aeroplanes approaching through the sky. Right above us, one unleashed its bombs. They fell slowly towards us, then gathered speed, exploding just a few hundred yards away. We were thrown back as the window-panes blew in.

A few days later we were huddled in the bomb shelter when the impact of the explosions blew its door off. Dust cascaded onto our heads. We emerged to find our house destroyed. We salvaged what we could and set off, by tram, by cart, to find a place to stay. Eventually we found two rooms and a kitchen at Olmeda, a hill village on the Como–Cantù line, some 30 miles from Milan. The area was full of refugees. My mother

---

[1] These are edited extracts from Rossana Rossanda's *La Ragazza del secolo scorso*, Einaudi: Turin 2007, paperback, 978 88 06 18816 0; they are printed by permission of the publisher.

worked for the office of an engineering firm that had been evacuated to Cantù; hers was the only regular income since my father had lost his business in Venice ten years before. I would take the tram back there from Milan in the evening, or stay at a friend's flat overnight.

One defeat followed another through the summer of 1943. The Allies had invaded Sicily but there was no 'defence of the fatherland'. Then, overnight, the regime collapsed. On July 25th Mussolini was under arrest, replaced by old Marshal Badoglio. Monarchists and Fascists fell to blaming each other; all of them—the King, the ministers, the Fascist leaders—were revealed as petty swindlers, the eagles and the laurel leaves as papier-mâché. I was stunned by the sudden dissolution of what had seemed such a powerful state machine. What did the Badoglio government mean? I pounced on the newspaper reports, dissatisfied and suspicious. The whole country seemed to be lying low, scared, wanting to get rid of the Germans, who were there and not there that summer. The first dissenting voices I heard were those of Giustizia e Libertà. The information they had was uncertain: papers, programmes, rumours. They were another sort of people, they seemed to take the measure of things according to a different set of dimensions.

September 1943

Badoglio had surrendered to the Allies. For less than a day we believed, with a kind of sad exultation, that it was the end of the war. It was the reverse: the King fleeing to the arms of the Allies in the South, the onset of German occupation in the North. Italy was broken in two like a loaf of bread. The long overcoats of the Germans were everywhere, their harsh orders posted on the walls. The atmosphere at the University was fraught with tension: it was time to choose—to side with the partisans, or to fight against the Allies under German command. The Italian Army had no credibility at all. We were all on our guard, careful who we spoke to, watching who was who.

Later, this period would be rewritten as one of national revolt against the Germans; but for us it was not a matter of patriotic enthusiasm. What national identity had Italy had before September 8th, 1943? The Risorgimento had involved the elites, not much more; if fascism had provided an identity, it had collapsed. We had been a state for two-and-a-half generations; what kind of national tradition starts—at best—with one's grandparents? The Italians were a precarious people, never tested by the choices it had to make, whether at the time of the Reformation, the French Revolution, or later revolts; the melting pot had never resulted in a fusion. Now, in 1943, the choice was not between Brindisi—where the King had fled—and Mussolini's lair in Desenzano. We had to decide whether to stay with the Italy we knew or work for its collapse: for an end to that Italy which had blurred the border between fascism and non-fascism, and would just have carried on doing so, without the war.

I don't know how I came to the conclusion that it was the Communists who were most sure of what they were doing—or who told me, 'But Banfi is a Communist'. I was so ignorant that I marched straight up to him, between classes. He was leaning against a radiator in the common-room, next to the window. 'Someone said you are a Communist.' He looked at me. I had taken two courses with him; he must have decided that I was what I seemed—someone in need of direction, who had no idea of the lethal import of what she had just said. 'What are you look-ing for?' I told him about the leaflets I'd seen, about being confused, not knowing. He got up from the radiator, went to the desk and wrote down a list in his tiny handwriting. 'Read these books. Come back when you have done so.' I ran to the railway station and opened the slip of paper on the train: Harold Laski, *Liberty in the Modern State* and *Democracy in Crisis*; Karl Marx, *The Eighteenth Brumaire of Louis Bonaparte* and *The Class Struggles in France 1848–1850*. A book by De Ruggiero, I think. Lenin, *State and Revolution*. 'By S., anything you can find.'

I was astounded. He really was a Communist—a Bolshevik. The images from Spain came into my head. I got off the train at Como and went to the public library. There was a kindly, middle-aged librarian. I showed him the list. He pointed me towards an old filing cabinet. The bottom drawer was unmarked, as if it were empty. I pulled it open. Everything was there, even *Das Kapital*, an Avanti! edition with a red leather cover. Nothing by S.; the only work on the USSR was a travel book by an engi-neer. I filled out the forms and the librarian brought me the books. 'May I take them home?' He nodded.

The evening tram back to Olmeda was crowded with people going home after work. Next to me were three exhausted labourers, with coarsened hands and blackened fingers. They looked as if they had been drink-ing; their drooping heads jerked to each movement of the tram. It was with them that I would have to go. At home I read all through the night, the next day, and the next. From Laski I went on to *The Eighteenth Brumaire*, then *State and Revolution*. I ran a fever. Everything fell into place; it was not so much a discovery as an acceptance which I could no longer defer. It was the end of my well-ordered future, my praiseworthy ambition, my innocence.

I went back to see Banfi. 'I've read it all.' 'Everything?' I nodded: 'What should I do?' He gave me the name of a schoolteacher in Como. She was expecting me, a middle-aged woman with tawny hair and heavy-lidded eyes. She spoke calmly, with a slight drawl. 'You need a pseudonym,' she said. 'You will be called Miranda, alright?' Miranda: what an idiotic name. I was told to look after the sister of a prisoner whose escape was being organized: Luciano Raimondi, an extraordinary partisan. The sister was a middle-aged woman with a startled look. I brought her food, tried to keep her calm. I am not good at looking after people and I was bored, but the escape was a success. The heavy-lidded woman gave me the address of a suitcase shop in Como. The man there would tell me what to do next. He was the centre of operations, I was to work with him. I went that evening. The little suitcase shop was tucked away in a side street. A customer was being served. After he had gone I stepped forward. 'I am Miranda.' The man behind the counter had grey hair, a serious face and clear eyes. He looked at me, questioningly. We were each putting our life into the other one's hands. Many go through life without ever experiencing this kind of relationship, which has no equal; but we did, then and later, wherever we went. His name was Remo Mentasti.

Resistance

By the autumn of 1943 the deportations were no longer disguised as 'work in Germany'. Lorries packed with deportees were driven away in the middle of the night; we heard about the round-up in the former ghetto in Rome. I was often afraid. I never knew whether or not I was being watched. In Milan there were always freshly posted proclamations on the walls from the German military governor, Field Marshal Kesselring, warning that we could be hanged. The thought filled me with horror. We saw the hanged in the public squares: their twisted necks, their elongated limbs. It was not death in itself; we had grown accustomed to that, walking with lowered heads, acknowledging it as something always there. It was the fact that the dead still bore the traces of what they had gone through, like the pile of bodies stacked, spread-eagled, their mouths and eyes wide open, in Milan's central square. The German and Italian forces kept them there all through a sweltering August day. It was as though we were being made to repudiate ourselves, forced to recognize that we dare not stand beside them and shout out, 'Me, too'.

Every non-vital question was put off till tomorrow. I tried to piece together the bits of information that came my way: Gasparotto dead, Curiel murdered, the botched contacts, the reprisals.[2] At the same time, I kept up with my studies. Banfi had assigned me a thesis on the aesthetic treatises of the early Renaissance and I was enchanted by the theorizations of light and perspective. And there was a love affair, the only thing that allowed me to imagine a life after the war, just as it taught me not to expect too much; we were trapped inside a cruel and indecisive time. What did it mean to be fifteen in 1939 and twenty-one in 1945? I still feel awkward about not having had a normal youth, not having danced through a single summer. It has made me anxious; probably boring, too.

As well as the luggage shop in Como there were several centres in Milan: street-corner rendezvous, coffeeless cafés, safe houses; and the University. Professor Banfi lived in Corso Magenta and it was natural enough to stroll with one's teacher along the Via Passione to the station. From Banfi I knew about the CLNAI—the Committee for the National Liberation of Northern Italy. Banfi was the only person who would answer all my questions. It was he who told me that Curiel had been shot, by an infiltrator; there were many of them in our ranks.

Sometimes it would get late, the curfew would be about to sound and I would not know what to do with the material I was carrying. At such moments, the people one could not approach seemed innumerable, and the comrades very scarce and far away. A few things accumulated at home: never guns or money, but medicine, cyclostyled leaflets that I had not managed to deliver, old sheets that Mimma and I cut into strips for bandages, rolled up tight. One morning my mother came bouncing into our room very early, in her vest. 'I've got a cold, do you have a handkerchief?' She opened a drawer: 'What is all this stuff?' There were bandages, medicines, heaven knows what. I was dumbstruck, but

---

[2] [Leopoldo Gasparotto (1902–44): fought in Lombardy with the anti-fascist group Giustizia e Libertà; Eugenio Curiel (1912–45): PCI militant, ran the clandestine *Unità* during the war and the Communist journal *La nostra lotta*.]

Mimma just shrugged it off: 'So?' Our mother may have thought this was just part of our disorderly nature; she shut the drawer and left.

One evening the train to Como was stopped by the Fascist militia, deep in the snowy countryside. Italian voices ordered us to get out with our luggage and stand in line to be searched. I was carrying material for the Brigade section in Val di Lanzo. The third-class compartment was packed with tired people, some standing, some sitting on the long wooden benches. Under their eyes, I slipped the big bag under the seat beneath me. I could not take it out. Nobody said anything. We lined up alongside the carriage. Some militiamen came by with a girl they had arrested, her face ashen. 'What will you do with her?' 'Nothing. She will go to Germany to work.' They looked through our belongings. They did not search inside the carriage. When we got back on the bag was still there. Nobody said a word. Getting out at Como it seemed as if they were all in a hurry to get away from me.

Another time our building in Olmeda was evacuated by the Germans in the middle of the night. They said they were searching for explosives that the partisans had put in a disused railway tunnel that ran beneath. I knew there was no gelignite there, but of course could not say so. As we stood in the cold and dark, wrapped in blankets, I felt some of the others were giving me fearful looks. But though they thought they might be blown up at any minute, no one said anything.

They did not speak, but people were watchful. The Germans could not tolerate the fact that the partisans—*Banditen*—were contending with them for control of territory; but in a country without hope, a guerrilla war is unbeatable. That was why the Germans were so merciless during the round-ups, why they continued to massacre during their retreat. We did not know about the camps, but we saw them at work, their helmets sloping down over their eyes, and we feared them. War against the Germans—or against the Fascists, and therefore civil war? I was amazed at the scandal that exploded later around Claudio Pavone's book, *Una guerra civile*.[3] It was obvious that it was both. Who if not Italians—the King, Mussolini, the Fascists—had brought us to this point? Who if not the Italian ruling class had handed us to the Germans? Daniel

---

[3] [Claudio Pavone, *Una guerra civile: saggio storico sulla moralità nella Resistenza*, Turin 1991.]

Guérin's *Fascism and Big Business* was an important work for us; patently, the two were linked.[4]

1944

Did we want a revolution? I rack my brains. We were Communists, we wanted a new country, but we were not preparing for an insurrection. Not where I was, in Milan, even if—I later found out—some of the partisan brigades had hopes of it, both encouraged and restrained by the elusive Secchia.[5] But radical words and radical deeds are different things. For us, to be a Communist was, above all, to be the most decisive in action—though I got to know some very determined monarchist officers. Those who joined the Party during the Resistance were a particular type, formed during that epoch: decisive, but also resolutely realistic.

On the few occasions that I had dealings with people from other parties in the CLNAI, I felt ill at ease. A heavy-browed Liberal lawyer, a former Deputy, received me with palpable fear. His was the only request that I refused. The Fascist Federale of Como—I think he was called Scassellati—needed someone to look after his daughter in the afternoons. I looked the part, I could pretend to be a Fascist, they could supply me with recommendations. I would listen, pass on information. 'Snoop? No', I said, immediately. The Deputy did not insist. Soon after I did pass on military documents to the Allies. But that was not like going into someone's house, winning their trust and then abusing it. I did not want to play the Mata Hari.

The Party cell structure was very rigid: my contacts were limited to one comrade here, one there, to guarantee the security of the network. As well as Mentasti in Como there was Dionisio, leader of the factory section at Cantù, the largest in the region. Dionisio was younger than Mentasti and more daring; a worker, but nothing like the tired figures I had seen on the tram. Even the older workers I met were not like that. They were watchful, men of few words, as if the practice of clandestinity had become a habit. Though there was nothing much about class strategies in the pamphlets that we managed to print off and distribute, there was always something to be learnt from the older workers: fragments

---

[4] [Daniel Guérin, *Fascisme et grand capital*, Paris 1936.]
[5] [Pietro Secchia (1903–73): PCI militant, political commissar of Communist Garibaldi Brigades during the war.]

of life, struggles, trade unions broken up, comrades imprisoned. From them I learnt of the splits in the Left in the 1930s. But I knew little of the trials of 1937, and of Gramsci, only the name.

In January 1944 the Americans had informed us they could not guarantee air drops during the winter: perhaps it would be better if the partisans came down from the mountains? As if a guerrilla war was an optional trip to the countryside. We were an occupied country, the Germans were hunting down the *Banditen*; those who had gone to fight with the Brigades could not just stroll back home. But the air supplies were not essential, or so it seemed to me. It was the networks in the cities that supplied those in the mountains. General Alexander's communiqué meant that the Allies would not be arriving any time soon; we had to fend for ourselves.

The CLNAI leadership could take comfort from world developments: the Normandy landings, the Liberation of Paris. Coming and going from Milan to Como, I had no such broader view. I made a mistake. There was a girl at the University who used to talk to us and sometimes lend a hand: a beautiful blue-eyed blonde. Once I asked her to look after something for me. We had managed to set up an operation against the Decima MAS unit at Brunate.[6] They had designs for some new craft, a sailor was going to get me copies of the plans; he had a pass for Switzerland and could get away across the border. I collected the plans and handed them on. It was a day in early October and it seemed sensible for me to disappear for the afternoon. I cycled to Venegono, near Varese, where I could read a hard-to-find Leon Battista Alberti volume in the Caproni Library. Towards evening, as I was cycling home, the blonde girl intercepted me in the central square in Como. Her face was drained of colour. 'Don't go home. I've warned your father'. It turned out she was involved with a German official and had informed him about me. She said I should make a run for it. I was so shocked I could barely take in what she was saying. It was the first and last time in my life that I ever hit somebody—my hand moved of its own accord.

As soon as I had told the comrades I pedalled home at top speed, terrified that my family would have been arrested. I found my father deathly pale.

---

[6] [Decima Flottiglia MAS: unit of frogmen, used against Allied shipping during the war and, on land, against partisans.]

'I have burned everything I could find in your room,' he said, briefly. 'Is there anything else?' 'No.' 'Who are you with?' 'The Communists.' 'Not the worst,' he said, almost relieved. *Meno male*—I have never understood what he meant by that. Three Germans arrived, two in uniform and a plainclothes officer, a figure of fear in Como. They found nothing. My father and I answered the few questions they put to us. They did not arrest me. As soon as they left my father asked: 'Why didn't you tell me?' 'You wouldn't have let me do it.' It was true, but then I added, 'I would do it again and not tell you anything.' It was cruel of me, not casual like the pain I have happened to inflict at other times. He winced, and left the room. It was the end of the long love between us, the special trust I had in him; the father who gave me books, who discussed all the big questions with me, all the things that mattered. He distanced himself from me and died, two years later, without us ever having talked the same way again.

I have no idea why I was not arrested. Possibly the Germans were after the Decima MAS documents themselves—there were tense relations between the two—and let me go in the hope of turning up some more important connection. That was the comrades' hypothesis, when we were able to speak. In the meantime I was isolated and guilt-stricken. People in Milan looked past me when I saw them in the street. I was summoned by the CLNAI a month later. Fabio was waiting for me in the crowd at Milan's northern railway station; later I would know him as Vergani, secretary of the city's Camera del lavoro. He was a calm, middle-aged man. Without raising his voice, he asked me whether I realized that I had put the whole network in danger by failing to follow an elementary rule. It was a simple and effective dressing-down. I felt a complete fool. His face conveyed what he thought but did not say: the problems that having to work with people like me created for the Resistance.

Vergani indicated that I would be given a signal when relations could resume. It came soon enough; the Germans started to leave the Como area that winter. In Milan there was a new wind blowing. The strikes of March 1945 were strong and almost happy: there were no trams running from Piazza Cadorna and many of the shops were shut. Bulletins from the mountains sounded a completely different note to those of the winter before: many were now going to join the partisans.

It was ending, but the losses were still severe. The short-lived Free Republic of Ossola was crushed by the Germans; the image of the hanging bodies with the signs around their necks at Fondotoce remained.[7] Then came April 28th, Mussolini's capture by the partisans as he tried to flee with the Germans. The official press and the radio went crazy. Everyone was talking: this was it. We heard about the negotiations that Cardinal Schuster—a sort of Milanese Pius XII—tried to broker. On May 5, the partisans marched through Milan. I saw Parri for the first time in the Piazza Duomo, marching next to Longo.[8] They were in civilian clothes. There was a kind of pride and happiness that I had never known before, nor ever would again. All around there were crowds of joyous people, climbing onto the monuments, scaling the lampposts. It was the same in Como, in Olmeda: the Italian tricolour was flying everywhere and people that you would have avoided the month before now had red scarves around their necks. It was the end of an epoch. Everything would start again.

I saw the bodies, Mussolini, Clara Petacci and the others, strung up by their feet in Piazzale Loreto. They looked done for, their faces swollen and anonymous as if they had never lived. Someone had tied Petacci's skirt up around her knees, out of pity. In front of them there thronged a furious mass of people, women shouting, men white-faced with indignation, screaming out their anger and their impotence: justice had been done by somebody else, on their behalf. There was some derision, but mostly rage. I turned away; it was a necessary ritual, perhaps, but terrible.

Liberation

There is no such thing as a clean war. We came out of it bruised and battered and could not just march away home, like the Russians or the Americans. A civil war does not end at an appointed hour, but only when enough time has passed to leave behind those who will never be able

---

[7] [On 20 June 1944, 42 partisans were executed at Fondotoce. The Free Republic of Ossola lasted for 43 days that autumn.]

[8] [Ferruccio Parri (1890–1981): member of CLNAI, Prime Minister of a unity government June–December 1945; Luigi Longo (1900–80): among founder members of PCI, commander of Garibaldi Brigades 1943–45; succeeded Togliatti as secretary of the Party, 1964–72.]

to forget. There were plenty of reprisals in the aftermath, some petty enough; some—like the case of Neri, a partisan leader, and Gianna, a slightly crazy girl—matters of conscience. Gianna had come down from the mountains a few times and once she was arrested in Como, but released after a few weeks. The partisans suspected her of having talked. Neri defended her. A partisan court, some of them people I knew, condemned the pair and they were executed—shot. I learnt of it from Remo Mentasti, who was in despair. He asked me to intervene, to make sure, at least, that the slur of treason was lifted. I called for an inquiry through the leadership in Milan, but came up against a brick wall; everyone did. Maybe the partisans did not want to admit their mistake; maybe they understood it was unpardonable. When the story of Neri and Gianna was resurrected in the 1970s I did not intervene. In 1945, nothing about that story had convinced me, but I did not think about leaving. I am not proud of it; nor repentant.

The Brera Picture Gallery had reopened and that winter we unpacked the books for its archive, hurriedly crated away during the Allied attacks. We worked amid jubilant disorder, stopping to read squatting on our heels as the precious volumes came to hand. There was a sense of movement in the air; painters, writers, photographers congregated at the Bar Giamaica outside the Brera. I graduated on February 6th, 1946. On February 7th I found a job, editing for the Hoepli Encyclopedia, and that evening I enrolled in the local branch of the Communist Party. It is not easy to recapture the way we thought then, buried as it is under the century's rubble. We were sure—I was sure—that only socialism, an end to the rule of big capital, would bring freedom from oppression, colonialism, fascism, war. Yet there was no expectation of imminent revolution, as there had been after the First World War. We were visibly, if amicably, occupied by the Americans, to whom the partisans had had to surrender arms. In 1945 the most compelling need was to put everything back in motion, to rebuild: Milan was devastated, the country was desperately poor. We had been cut off from the world for twenty years under Fascism; before that there had been the frivolous *Italietta* of the belle époque. The 20th century had been denied to us and now we tore into it like hungry young leopards—not just American and Soviet culture, but the whole of modern Europe. We discovered the art of the 20s and 30s amid the rubble of the postwar era: the books—my heart stopped when I picked up Marcel Raymond's *De Baudelaire au surréalisme*: a work long sought comes to seem the key to every lock—the music: the first Marion Anderson 78s, the first *swing*; the films; the theatre. We were swept away, and at first did not notice the re-imposition of censorship, this time by the Church.

It was a time of ferment; there was a wonderful gaiety in the air. The main office of the Einaudi publishing house in Viale Tunisia was a meeting place for all sorts of writers and editors, who read, published, ate and slept there—Giulio Einaudi, Pavese, Calvino, Cerati,[9] Vando Aldrovandi. I am still embarrassed to recall the first talk I did for them, on Hemingway; I hardly knew what to say. At midnight we used to go to *L'Unità*'s office in the Piazza Cavour, to pick up the first edition of the next day's paper. Elio Vittorini was still the editor there, though soon he would leave, following a tirade from Togliatti, and set up *Il Politecnico*. If the name recalled that of Carlo Cattaneo's 19th-century journal of Piedmontese revolutionary-republicanism—in contradistinction to the Roman line of descent, from Labriola, Croce, Gramsci—what Vittorini and the others were really thinking of was Paris, New York, 1920s Berlin.[10] It was the first clash—pitting not so much practical party men against intellectuals, but two ideas, political as well as intellectual: Milan and Rome. We stressed the links between Communism and modernity, Communism and the avant-garde; Rome and Naples, those between Communism and national formation, Italian tradition. We were more interested in big industry, Rome in the peasant struggles of the South against the latifundia. Florence was in between, with Luporini and Muscetta's journal *Società*; or so it seemed to us at the time.[11]

Rome did not understand, we told ourselves, with a presumption that consorted all too well with a certain opportunism; for among the northern intelligentsia there was a feeling—not least among non-Communists, as a legacy from the joint Resistance—that it was necessary to keep in step with the backwardness of the South. (And I was taken aback by how narrowly the referendum on Republic or Monarchy passed in the

---

[9] [Roberto Cerati: an editor at Einaudi from 1945.]
[10] [The original *Il Politecnico* was founded by Cattaneo in Milan in 1839 as a journal of revolutionary republicanism. Vittorini's was published between September 1945 and December 1947.]
[11] [*Società*: founded in 1945 by a group of Communist intellectuals including Cesare Luporini and Carlo Muscetta; ceased publication in 1961.]

summer of 1946, despite the ridiculous spectacle of the runaway King.[12])
So Milan stood aside, so to speak. Vittorini withdrew from *L'Unità*. Banfi
nearly had to shut down *Studi Filosofici* after protestations from the
French Communists over its defence of Sartre against Jean Kanapa's
attack. On the broader question of education, however, there was still
a mutual understanding. Neither the enlightenment tradition nor the
avant-garde were 'popular', but for a while that did not seem to be the
most important problem. The people had been cut off, excluded; access
to culture was a matter of privilege. There was no concession to pop-
ulism and provincialism, but rather a common assumption that neither
people nor culture could stay the same.

The Communists and Socialists of those days came in many stripes. The
Socialists of Milan had an aura of heresy about them, thanks to Lelio
Basso and Ricardo Lombardi, both of them somewhat suspect in Rome:
the first for being Luxemburgist when no one else was, the second for
having proposed a flat tax on shares when Rome was very careful not to
create any trouble for Bresciani Turroni at the Constituent Assembly.[13]
Rodolfo Morandi was regarded with suspicion by the PCI for raising the
question of workers' self-management councils after the war.[14] But the
Milan region failed to provide any great national political leaders, least
of all on the Left. The only Lombards who counted on the national scene
were products of Milan's Banca Commerciale, which stood in splendour
opposite the run-down Palazzo Marino, the City Hall. The Socialist Mayor,
Antonio Greppi, with his perpetually heartfelt expression, sat behind
an ugly desk awaiting its resurrection while the Banca Commerciale's
saturnine chief, Raffaele Mattioli—who maintained close relations with
Togliatti and Piero Sraffa, via Franco Rodano—was elegantly enthroned
in the building across the street, with a stack of not-at-all financial books

---

[12] [In June 1946 the Italian referendum decided for the Republic by 12 million to
10 million, with the South favouring a monarchy. Although the parties of the Left
won 219 seats in the 1946 Constituent Assembly election, compared to 207 for the
Christian Democrats, Togliatti and Nenni accepted minority roles in De Gasperi's
coalition government, which retained the Lateran Treaty with the Vatican and the
Fascist penal code.]
[13] [Basso (1903–78): PSI member and Resistance fighter; edited Italian edition of
Luxemburg's *Political Writings* published in 1967. Lombardi (1901–84): Resistance
fighter, joined PSI in 1947. Costantino Bresciani Turroni (1882–1963): economist,
appointed head of Bank of Rome in 1945.]
[14] [Rodolfo Morandi (1903–55): militant in Giustizia e Libertà and PSI in Milan.]

on the table.[15] Nearby, in an ex-workingmen's club in Via Rovello, was the Piccolo Teatro where Giorgio Strehler and Paolo Grassi were initiating an Italian version of Jean Vilar's Théâtre National Populaire. There was enormous confusion. Milan was still full of potholes and rubble, there were barely any streetlights, crime was rife; but everything was safer than during the war. Compared to the Kesselring posters, the piles of dead, the hanged—we could live with the peace.

Party work

By February 1946, when I enrolled in my local branch of the PCI, the membership had changed. The clandestine network and the partisans had been submerged within a broader layer. I recognized some who had toiled away during the war, but there were many who had not, who had submitted to events under the Germans but who were now looking for a bearing. It surprised me that the doors were so wide open, the procedures for admission almost non-existent. It was certainly not the party of Lenin.

It was then that I discovered the world of the big industrial plants: not the little workshops of Cantù or Brianza, but the high walls and vast assembly shops of Innocenti, Alfa and Borletti in Milan; of Breda, Marelli and Falck in Sesto San Giovanni. Typically, the entrance to these factory gates would be ploughed to mud by truck tyres and the tramping of feet, as if the city had pulled back twenty yards from the plant, or vice versa. The factories always had a half-built look: concrete and corrugated iron behind the wooden frontages or the fretwork of the 1900s. Until the Olivetti buildings in Ivrea, there was no sign of the modern movement: the factory was not architecture, just a container. The only beauty lay in the machines; an oily rag among the steel rods was the trace of a worker who would help the parts move to a smoother beat, a tempo of their own.

We went there with the Party paper, to discuss and to recruit. At first some of the big factories were open to us, and we would set up shop in the plant's trade-union office, or wait for the workers to come out into the chilly sunshine at midday to eat what they had brought from home.

---

[15] [Franco Rodano (1920–83): Catholic anti-fascist, part of wartime Movimento dei Cattolici Comunisti.]

At Innocenti, the workers' management council seemed to run the company. It was led by Muneghina, a highly intelligent comrade with a biting Lombardy wit. He amused himself by running after us with the big hook that hung from an aerial chain, sometimes hoisting us up into the air on it for a few yards. For the workers, the factories they had defended from transfer or sabotage during the German retreat seemed rightfully theirs—and therefore ours; Italy's. The women workers—grey-faced, with drawn features and iron-clad perms—were harder to get to talk to. They were always in a rush, hurrying to clock in on time in the morning, hurrying out to buy milk before the shops closed, or hurrying home to prepare the next day's lunch box at night. When the factory siren sounded the whole workforce would rush towards the trams, for the city's reconstruction had expelled them to the outer suburbs and they travelled in every morning in carriages befogged with breath and steam.

Party meetings were held in the evenings, often in the basements of the old council estates that formed a big belt around Milan, outside the *case di ringhiera*, the 'banister houses'. On one side of those courtyards there would be a door marked with the hammer and sickle, or a notice of the last meeting. Down a few steps, and you would be in the entrails of the building, with pipes running everywhere, the walls repainted by decorator comrades and the table covered with lengths of red cloth that would be carefully folded and put away at the end of the meeting. Often the room was completely full but more people would come hesitantly down the stairs, curious to see what the Communists were like, and end up perching at the back. The branch secretary's report would begin with a summary of the world situation, followed by a survey of international and domestic events, and an account of decisions taken by the leading bodies and the Central Committee; it covered everything down to the branch telephone bill. Of course there was something schematic in the transposition from world stage to Milanese suburb, from historical event to the corresponding Party resolution; but it was an enormous acculturation.

The report was followed by a discussion, which was never very long, or much of a debate. When someone took the floor to challenge the Party line—always from the Left, arguing that the Togliatti leadership was making too many concessions—others sprang reflexively to its defence, and not only from the speakers' table: anything to avoid dividing that embryo of another Italy that joined people together, saving them from the isolation of the big city, the factory floor. This was the solid real-ity of the party that was slowly worn down in the 1970s and 80s, and destroyed by the political changes of 1989; a tired but living network that organized people of the left within another tradition, counter-posed to the homogenization of the mass media.

The people who packed the basement meetings, tired after the day's work, or went from door to door getting membership cards stamped, were workers, teachers, engineers, some students; mostly poor, though not all; and neatly dressed—where there was real poverty there was no *faux* pauperism. Although exploited and oppressed, they had the sim-plicity and self-confidence that came from being sure they understood, better than most, the laws that made the world go round. And since they were convinced that they always fell below their own ideals, they were also moralistic, stern with others and with that part of the self which risked being the other. I came down like the rest, listened, spoke occa-sionally, took on my share of the tasks. I learnt a lot. I was not always persuaded, but that seemed normal to me. I was no longer an adoles-cent, I did not seek or find a form of religiosity there. My formation was one thing; that of the speaker, or of those sitting next to me, was another. I never thought they had to coincide. This was the Party I belonged to in the postwar period.

In the cold

The bright days proved shortlived. In May 1947 De Gasperi broke up the postwar coalition, evicting the Left parties from government. The branch secretary's report had as its background Churchill's speech at Fulton, then the Truman doctrine. The Allies were pitted against each other, and we felt the brunt of the Cold War in our daily lives. The ground was shifting under our feet; we were thrown on to the defensive and had to get used to the police breaking up our meetings, beating us up; though if they got penned into a courtyard, they could get thrashed themselves. The judiciary went on the rampage, armed with the Rocco Code. Soon we needed a permit even for indoor meetings, and when a dispute started in a factory stones would fly and windows shatter.

The April 1948 elections were a turning point. I doubt De Gasperi believed his own propaganda, that the Communists and Socialists would impose a godless dictatorship, that we were just waiting for the right moment to liquidate democracy. He was intelligent and well-informed enough to know that, in those times and with all those American bases, a revolution in Italy was not conceivable. But he feared our strength, our influence. In reality, it was the PCI that risked being ruled out of the democratic process, and many in Milan and Lombardy thought that if the Left won it would be the bourgeois state that would overturn the vote.

It was my first, terrifying electoral campaign. The villages of lower Lombardy glide past in my memory. Every time the car deposited me in one of those squares, my stomach knotted: what am I doing here? I would launch myself at the audience in a cold sweat, scrutinizing the serious, impassive faces, workers and others, farmhands in their overalls, to see if the 'girl from Milan' could make them feel they were not alone. It was a strange sensation. We were strong, the only organized party; but surrounded by a sea of priests and madonnas, whose gilded statues were taken from place to place to exorcize our baleful influence. The vote count was terribly slow, it went on for days. The first few provincial seats went to the Christian Democrats, then those in the towns; and then the flood—DC, DC, DC. After a third of the votes had been counted, the DC were far ahead of us. We couldn't believe it. Even in the working-class districts, we came in below the most pessimistic forecasts. It was a hard blow, a decisive defeat that would install the Christian Democrats as the dominant political presence for decades to come. We were out of government, the permanent opposition—even when the PCI began to score a large plurality of the vote. We did not know then about the *conventio ad excludendum,* keeping the Communists out of any Italian government; that would be formalized later, in step with the struggle between the two superpowers, the creation of NATO, the sordid conspiracies of Operation Gladio.

New spring

The 1960s were more interesting. In Italy these were years of rising labour struggles, of chaotic urban growth. For us, 1968 began in 1967, in the Architecture Departments of Turin and Venice; exploded in Trento with the occupation of the Sociology Faculty, and spread nearly everywhere from December throughout 1968. I was fighting the government's disastrous university legislation in Parliament when the student movement began to take off. I plunged into the protests, all the more sympathetic to the students' demands because of the disparagement we had started to receive within the PCI for raising criticisms of the Communist leadership—over the 20th Party Congress, Hungary, the Sino-Soviet split.[16] Meanwhile, the international scene was in tumult, and it all seemed part of the same wave: Hanoi resisted the American escalation and went onto the counter-attack, and it was clear the Soviet Union was providing material support; Dubček was trying to put in place a form of socialist democracy; while China was actively posing the question of what post-revolutionary society was. The PCI leadership had sided with the Soviet Union since 1960, and could see nothing in the Cultural Revolution but a struggle for power at the top of the CCP—i.e., nothing at all. The films of Godard and Bellocchio registered the historical scale of the Chinese turmoil far more powerfully than did the Central Committee.

Everything began to pick up speed: Vietnam, Czechoslovakia, China. Europe watched in a daze as its youth came out onto the streets, articulating things that had never been said before. At the beginning of May Nanterre erupted, rapidly spreading to Paris and becoming a symbol for the whole world. Within weeks, France was paralysed by a general strike. I went with friends; we camped at K. S. Karol's house, went down to the barricaded Latin Quarter and spent the first evening at the Odéon, packed like sardines. Everyone had the right to take the floor. 'Let them speak!' was the cry when someone stumbled, struggling to express the subjectivity of atomization. By June, as we made our way back to Milan, the clouds were already beginning to gather over Prague. Around midnight on August 21st Alfredo Reichlin phoned me from *L'Unità*: Soviet tanks were entering the city. Karol and I ran to the Cuban embassy. The ambassador was expecting the condemnation from Havana at any moment. The next morning Reichlin called me again: 'Your friend Castro is not condemning the invasion.' The days that followed were feverish. In Prague the Soviet troops were greeted with incredulity; unlike in Budapest, there was no resistance. When the Czechs berated the soldiers who stuck their heads out of the turrets: 'But why are you here?', they did not know what to reply.

---

[16] [On PCI debates in this period, see articles by Perry Anderson, 'Debate of the Central Committee of the Italian Communist Party', NLR 1/13–14, January–April 1962; Lucio Magri, 'Italian Communism in the Sixties', NLR 1/66, March–April 1971; Luciana Castellina, '*Il Manifesto* and Italian Communism', NLR 1/151, May–June 1985.]

There was uproar at the PCI's 12th Party Congress in February, the first since the invasion. The leadership's document was ambivalent on everything: students, the internal situation, Prague. I was the first of our group to take the microphone: 'We are gathered here while the army of a country that calls itself socialist is occupying another socialist country'. Bam!—the entire Soviet delegation got up and left, led by Ponomariov, who had been at my place in Milan often enough. The other delegations followed suit—all except the Vietnamese; we thought this significant at first, until we found out they were having problems with the translation. The silence from the presidium was glacial, but there was a huge ovation from the floor. It was the same when Aldo Natoli spoke, attacking the PCI's lukewarm attitude towards the social struggles; and Luigi Pintor, who assailed the ossification and authoritarianism of the inner-Party regime. By the end of the third day we knew how strong our support was, although far fewer would vote for a document we put up against the leadership's theses—so as not to divide the Party; so as not to expose ourselves, as a minority; all the usual reasons. I was the only one with a voice on the Policy Commission who could argue for permission to put our document to the Congress; we got the go-ahead. We would get a derisory amount of votes—but still.

Then Berlinguer spoke—the inauguration of his de facto leadership.[17] He acknowledged in passing several of the points we had been raising— though nothing about the Soviet Union. But the Congress delegates saw it as a possible opening towards our views. The few comrades who had wanted to vote for our document all clustered round me, their faces friendly, worried: they wanted to put their faith in the new General Secretary. I presented the document to the Congress, and explained why we would not be putting it to a vote. Not a glorious moment. My uneasiness was increased by the sudden warmth of the applause all around me, for declining to take an oppositional stand. I left the podium, picked up my bag, and walked out of the hall.

The next two months were unbearable. How could so much conservatism have accumulated within the Party? It still seemed something new—it was not predetermined that the Party would respond to 1968 by withdrawing into its shell. As for the Soviet Union, it was not even capable of keeping its own camp in order without the use of arms. It had

---

[17] [Enrico Berlinguer (1922–84): PCI militant from 1943 onwards; general secretary of the Party from 1972 until his death.]

nothing to say on what was to be done in the ex-colonial countries, and limited itself to supporting a dubious progressivism in the Middle East. It was no longer a besieged fortress, yet still exhausted itself pursuing the arms race; and all the time undermining itself from within. By 1969, nothing could be hoped for unless there was a profound change in the Soviet leadership; the masses had become anaesthetized—not through terror, through scepticism. As for the Italian Party, the living body to which I had linked myself since 1943, with whom I had travelled all these years—what stage of suffering, of desire and powerlessness, had it now reached? I had grown used to operating within it as if playing on a great keyboard, one that registered my touch and sent messages in response. Now I had been distanced from its keys. But we had not given up on the Party: there was still the hope that we had lost a battle, but not the war. Why not go on the attack, launch a new monthly journal? We had nothing to lose.

The idea of *Il Manifesto* came first and foremost from Lucio Magri. Pintor, Natoli, Luciana Castellina, Eliseo Milani and I were with him from the outset, others came on board once it got started. We found a small publisher in Bari. Our blood was starting to pulse once more. Out of fairness we had to keep the Party informed. I was sent to speak to Berlinguer: 'We're starting a monthly review. I haven't come to get advice, because you'd say no; I have come to let you know'. He did not get angry with me, partly because he rarely lost control but also, perhaps, because he was thinking it through. He knew who we were and that we would get a hearing. 'Explain what you want to do.' I told him. He advised against, without much ardour; he understood that we had made up our minds. 'Do you think there will be any disciplinary sanctions?' I asked him. 'That I would exclude.' I took my leave, promising to show him the first proofs.

June 1969

We spent hours discussing the new journal's name before we finally settled on *Il Manifesto*—thinking of 1848. All of us wrote contributions for the first issue. I sent the proofs to Berlinguer, who rang me straight away: 'And you call this a journal of analysis? It's nothing but political interventions.' 'It's the same thing.' He asked me to postpone the launch for a fortnight, he wanted to attack the invasion of Czechoslovakia at the Moscow Congress and the last thing he needed was the CPSU waving our magazine in his face. Agreed. The first edition of *Il Manifesto* came out at the end of June and sold some 32,000 copies, soon rising to 80,000, making a small fortune for the Bari publisher. Berlinguer rang me several times in August. He did not want to expel us, and proposed a series of compromises: *Il Manifesto* could continue, but with someone from the leadership alongside us on the editorial board. It was not a route we could take. A journal is not an anthology.

It was Magri's editorial for the September 1969 *Il Manifesto*, after the first anniversary of the invasion of Czechoslovakia, that brought things to a head: 'Prague is Alone' argued that the Dubček course had been too much for Moscow, too little for Washington. All hell broke loose. The Central Committee was convened and formally requested *Il Manifesto* be shut down. The paradox was that the Italian 'Hot Autumn' of 1969 was just beginning. Instead of starting up as usual after the holidays, factory after factory was being occupied by the workers, with the massive Fiat plant in the lead. Yet the PCI was entirely concentrated on our case. The Hot Autumn was the largest, most sophisticated industrial struggle since the War—not just a strike, but a matter of the workers taking the entire production process into their own hands, elbowing the management hierarchy aside. And these were not an experienced cohort, tested by decades of repression, but young workers, often without qualifications, whose education had come from the chaotic development of the society they had grown up in; who had taken something from the resounding student protests of the year before and made it their own.

Was it revolution the young workers had in mind when they marched in through the factory gates and took over the assembly lines? The decision ran like a spark from plant to plant: they fought to change their work-place, to keep it in their hands. They shook off the habit of obedience. When they spoke in the assemblies, the union leaders had to queue up for the microphone like the least skilled worker, just as at the Odéon in Paris the year before—but without that sense of atomization. They were in their own place; they talked about how things had been done up till now, what they could not take, how things could be done. The stakes were very high; for capital there could hardly be a greater challenge.

The media knew it. At first they were pleased to see the PCI and the unions bypassed, then they were frightened. This was different from the university occupations the year before: not a children's rebellion, but a refusal of the only way the establishment could imagine factories being run. They were shocked that Fiat could be run by its subordinates, that factory workers could discuss production issues on the different assembly lines and come to an agreement, without the management having any say. If the students' mockery in 1968 was unpardonable, so too was the workers' unveiling of the shabby power mechanisms that underlay industrial production in the Hot Autumn of 1969. The more so since in occupying the factories the workers provided themselves with a platform, with the direct election of their delegates.

Autumn 1969 was, I think, the only time in the post-war era that the potential of a struggle at the heart of the system of production seemed— for a moment, was—unlimited. Europe was still shaken by 1968, the United States by the movement against the Vietnam War; echoes of the Chinese Cultural Revolution still reverberated. Latin America was in turmoil, torn between guerrilla warfare and military juntas. It was an acute crisis, in a common climate both universal and unorganized; a shudder that ran from one social sector to another. Only the Soviet Union was not traversed by the shocks of 1968 and 69; further proof of its sclerosis.

The explosion of 1969 was the rationale for *Il Manifesto*. The PCI could not have given leadership to that insurgency without besieging the means of production on an ever-expanding scale; it would need to take powers of decision over property without spurring a flight of capital. It was not easy—but nothing was tried, nothing was thought, not even one step forward from that Keynesian ambit in which the PCI had developed; and which would itself soon be overthrown. It is those years that explain the present. On November 24th, 1969 the Central Committee was reconvened to vote on our expulsion. The formula they used meant that we were not enemies, sell-outs or spies. It was just a difference of approach. Berlinguer told me that there would be no time limit on my intervention after the report. At the entrance to the hall he took me aside: 'There is still time.' 'To make a gesture of obedience?' 'No, a gesture of loyalty.' I spoke for about forty minutes, as did Aldo Natoli. They did not forgive his remark, 'You don't need a Party card to be a communist.'

No, you don't need a card to be a communist; but to lead a country you need a mass party. The PCI was not that party, or not any more. At least

Aldo and I never fooled ourselves into believing we could set up another in its stead. We at *Il Manifesto* were thrown out into the thick of the workers' struggles and the crisis in the universities. We hoped to be a bridge between the new hopes of the young and the knowledge of an older left that had had its hours of glory. It did not work out that way—but that's another story.

DENNIS RODGERS

A SYMPTOM CALLED MANAGUA

I N A FAMOUS essay entitled 'An Illness Called Managua', the Nicaraguan poet Pablo Antonio Cuadra contended that the city was paradigmatically 'the reflection of [Nicaraguan] society, of its grace and its bitterness, of its vice and its beauty, of its history and its community'.[1] Managua's recent development also provides a perspective on the dramatic transformations that the country has undergone over the past decades: from corrupt dictatorship through popular insurrection and social reconstruction, rapidly choked off by Cold War intervention and economic crisis, to a Miami-style restoration and a new growth model led by narco-trafficking and Free Trade Zones. A study of Managua's changing morphology and socio-economic trajectory suggests that the city is less an 'illness' than a symptom of this pathologized development path.

Sprawling along the southern shores of Lake Xolotlán, the city presents a strange landscape: a humid basin, filled with foliage and vacant lots, with sporadic developments thrown up apparently at random, punctuated by low hills and lagoons formed in the craters of extinct volcanoes. An eruption from one of these 10,000 years ago preserved the footprints of the site's first settlers in the *barrio* of Acahualinca—one of the earliest such settlements in the Americas. Prior to the Spanish Conquest in the 16th century, the region was inhabited by a mixture of indigenous groups who had migrated both from Mesoamerica and from lands to the south, but the demographic collapse wrought by colonialism meant that *mestizos* soon came to dominate in numerical terms. During the colonial era and for decades after Nicaraguan independence—formally declared in 1821, but only fully obtained in 1838, with the dissolution of the United Provinces of Central America—the country's principal cities were the colonial centres of León and Granada, respective headquarters of the feuding Liberal and Conservative factions of the oligarchy. Managua was designated Nicaragua's capital in 1852, as a compromise between the two, but it remained relatively marginal until the middle decades of the 20th century.[2]

It was under the dictatorship of Anastasio Somoza, head of the US-trained National Guard, that Managua assumed its national prominence. Somoza seized power in 1936, after murdering Augusto César Sandino and crushing the popular movement he had led against the 1912–33 US occupation of the country. Somoza established an authoritarian regime that was to prove Central America's most durable, and among its most kleptocratic. He and his sons ruled Nicaragua until the 1979 Revolution, operating through the military and political apparatus of the National Guard, manipulating government contracts and siphoning off loans and aid to secure a commanding position in the country's economic life. They eventually amassed a family fortune estimated at $500 million, as well as 1.2 million acres of landholdings and direct ownership of 200 companies.[3] Political stability was assured by a tacit pact between the Somozas and the traditional oligarchy, both Liberals and Conservatives, behind a constitutional façade, enabling all three groups to share the spoils, albeit unequally, during the growth years of the 1950s and 60s.[4]

Nicaragua's export earnings—gold, coffee, cotton—funded a degree of industrial expansion. The population of Managua rose to over a quarter of a million by 1960.[5] Its bustling downtown—the playground known as 'Salsa City'—was packed with bars, dance-halls and cinemas that became a magnet for wealthy tourists from all over North and South

---

[1] Pablo Antonio Cuadra, 'Una enfermedad llamada Managua', cited in *La Prensa*, 13 December 2002.

[2] In 1900 León's population of 30,000 was still larger than Managua's; Granada had declined, having been burnt to the ground in the 1850s by the US filibuster William Walker who, invited in by León's Liberals, briefly made himself President of the country.

[3] John Booth and Thomas Walker, *Understanding Central America*, Boulder, CO 1989.

[4] Francisco Mayorga, *Megacapitales de Nicaragua*, 2nd edition, Managua 2007, pp. 37–9.

[5] Bryan Higgins, 'The place of housing programs and class relations in Latin American cities: The development of Managua before 1980', *Economic Geography*, vol. 66, no. 4 (1990), p. 380.

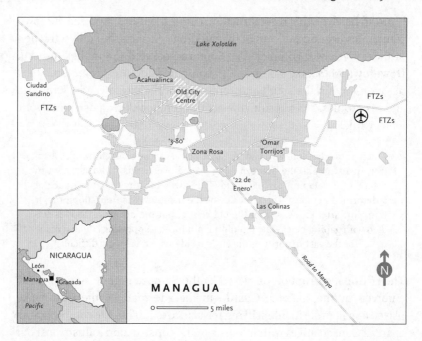

America. The majority of the population growth, however, occurred in the ever-expanding informal settlements on the city's periphery, as small tenant farmers were driven from the countryside by the mechanization of agriculture for export. The 60s boom also created a large if precarious urban middle stratum of small-scale entrepreneurs and shopkeepers, skilled service and white-collar workers, teachers, lower-rank administrative officials and so on, that made up nearly a fifth of Nicaragua's workforce by the early 1970s—layers that were highly exposed to arbitrary predations by the lower ranks of the Somoza clan's retinue and the National Guard.[6]

Managua's population had reached nearly half a million by 1972, when a devastating earthquake killed at least 10,000 people, destroyed 75 per cent of its housing, 90 per cent of its commercial buildings—including most of the centre—and left 300,000 homeless. Although international aid poured in to help rebuild Nicaragua's shattered capital, little reconstruction actually took place. Anastasio Somoza—younger son of the original dictator, who had been assassinated in 1956—appointed

---

[6] Harald Jung, 'Behind the Nicaraguan Revolution', NLR I/117, pp. 72–3.

himself head of the reconstruction committee and awarded his own companies over 80 per cent of the building contracts; but only a fraction of these were ever completed as Somoza pocketed the money himself. Downtown Managua was virtually abandoned and most rebuilding took place on land in the south and south-east of the city, owned by Somoza and his cronies.[7] As a result, 'the central core took on a post-apocalyptic look', while:

> Much of the development [that did take place] can be characterized as leap-frog in nature, as the Somoza gang leaped over lands it did not own in favour of developing parcels it did. This gives the city the appearance of a deformed octopus. The tentacles of the octopus reach out along major transport arteries away from the old centre, but the octopus's body is riddled with gaping holes. The rebuilding produced a sprawling city that made travel for the vast majority of the city's residents increasingly difficult.[8]

The criminal corruption displayed by the Somoza regime—and brutally enforced by the National Guard—in the aftermath of the earthquake played a major role in intensifying resistance to it. The elite compact came apart as Conservatives with interests in the construction industry lost out on their share of rebuilding contracts to the Somoza clan. Spiralling inflation, rising taxes and falling real wages brought the exposed small sectors of the economy to near collapse. Elite opposition, rallied in the UDEL, looked to the Carter Administration in Washington for support in ousting a dictator who had become such a patent liability.[9] But the Democratic Congress continued to vote military funding for the National Guard, and—even as the latter were subjecting the civilian population to aerial bombardment and artillery fire—Carter sent a personal letter to Somoza congratulating him on the human rights situation in his country.

The only force in Nicaragua capable of countering the aggressions of the National Guard was the ex-Guevarist Frente Sandinista de Liberación Nacional (FSLN), founded in 1961. By the mid-70s the Frente had abandoned their failed *foco* strategy and were attempting instead to

---

[7] Julio César Godoy Blanco, 'El proceso de estructuración urbana de Managua: 1950–1979', unpublished PhD dissertation, Department of Sociology, Universidad de Costa Rica 'Rodrigo Faccio', 1983.
[8] David Wall, 'City profile: Managua', *Cities*, vol. 13, no. 1 (1996), pp. 48–9.
[9] The Unión Democrática de Liberación (UDEL) was founded in 1974 by Pedro Joaquín Chamorro Cardenal, scion of a prominent Conservative family and editor of Nicaragua's leading newspaper *La Prensa*, in order to provide a focus for the burgeoning elite opposition to Somoza.

build mass urban bases, while continuing guerrilla actions against the National Guard. Their minimum programme was the nationalization of Somocista property—some 60 per cent of the economy—and the dissolution of the National Guard. From October 1977 the FSLN stepped up their attacks—temporary occupations of towns, holding political meetings, recruiting fighters, seizing weaponry—while seeking alliances with the Church and with the UDEL Conservatives. Meanwhile a 'Group of Twelve' bankers, industrialists, priests and university teachers from the Conservative elite declared that the FSLN had to be part of any solution; many of the sons and daughters of old Conservative families went to join the guerrilla. In late 1978 an FSLN-led insurrection was beaten back by the National Guard. A general strike was launched in June 1979. The FSLN took more territory, in fierce fighting. By July 1979 they had encircled Managua. Somoza fled to Miami on 17 July, and the FSLN took the capital two days later.

Sandinista city

Downtown Managua was still in ruins after the earthquake, and much of the city suffered terribly during the revolutionary uprising. Members of the new Sandinista government, installed in one of the remaining office blocks, looked out across the uncleared rubble.[10] The city's population had almost doubled since 1972, swollen by war and economic crisis; unemployment was estimated at 60 per cent and urban infrastructure had virtually collapsed. Capital flight in 1978 was estimated at $233 million and GDP shrank by 26 per cent in 1979 alone.[11] The FSLN-led junta nevertheless drew up ambitious plans to reconstruct and transform the city: creating a park in the old centre, planting trees, painting murals. Strategies were set in place to upgrade informal squatter settlements and rebuild infrastructure. With Cuban help, an overall building regulation plan was drawn up for the city in 1982 which laid out the framework for land use, establishing different zonal categories—residential, commercial, industrial, parkland, mixed—and stipulating restrictions concerning construction, population density and right of way.[12] Low-cost housing for the poor was a major priority: by 1983 over 8,000 serviced

---

10 Wall, 'Managua', p. 48.
11 Jung, 'Behind the Nicaraguan Revolution', p. 85.
12 The 1982 *Plan Regulador de Managua* prepared the way for a longer-term Urban Development Scheme (*Esquema de Desarrollo Urbano de Managua, 1987–2020*), drawn up in 1987 with technical assistance from the Cuban Central Planning Board, but never implemented due to lack of funds.

lots had been constructed in preparation for large-scale self-help house-building programmes.[13] It was on the basis of such initiatives that the Sandinistas won 66 per cent of the vote in the 1984 elections, despite the dire state of the economy and a developing civil war.

Only a few of the house-building programmes were ever completed, however. Former National Guard fighters had regrouped as *Contrarevolucionarios*, operating from bases in Honduras and heavily armed by the Reagan Administration. Fuelled by Washington's dollars, the Contras' ranks swelled from 500 in 1981 to 15,000 in 1986. The Sandinistas' ambitious development plans for Managua ground to a halt, as the state's meagre resources were re-channelled towards the pressing needs of food production and national defence, with an estimated 60 per cent of the budget going to the military by the middle of the decade. Contra terror and capital flight brought about a further contraction of the economy: direct damage from the Contra war was estimated at \$1 billion and its indirect economic costs at \$3 billion; the US economic embargo was illegally enforced by the mining of Nicaragua's harbours. The situation worsened still further after 1985, with the onset of world recession and rising interest rates; the national debt spiralled and hyperinflation took hold. In 1988 the FSLN themselves introduced draconian austerity measures: 50,000 public employees lost their jobs and wages fell to the level of the 1950s.

The impact on Managua was intensified by a massive influx of people displaced from the countryside by the war, in which some 30,000 Nicaraguans were killed. During the 1970s the annual rate of rural migration to the city averaged 28 per thousand; by the mid-1980s it was estimated at 46 per thousand—equivalent to almost 30,000 new inhabitants per year, most of them struggling to get by in the interstices of an impoverished informal economy.[14] There was an explosion of new squatter settlements, mainly on the city outskirts but some among the still uncleared downtown ruins—increasingly perceived as a symbol of the FSLN's failed attempts at urban reconstruction. Military conscription and war fatigue further undermined support for the FSLN, who were finally defeated by the Unión Nacional Opositora (UNO)—an eclectic

---

[13] See for example Ministerio de la Vivienda y Asentamientos Humanos (MINVAH), *Programa Integral de 2,800 Viviendas para Managua*, Managua 1980.
[14] Roberto Chavez, 'Urban Planning in Nicaragua: the First Five Years', *Latin American Perspectives*, vol. 14, no. 2 (1987), p. 234.

coalition of Liberals, Conservatives, and extreme left- and right-wing mini-parties—in the 1990 elections. The same year saw the installation of the Liberal Arnoldo Alemán as Managua's new mayor.

Elite backlash

The UNO government under Violeta Chamorro (1990–97) pushed through an immediate programme of privatizations. Of the 370 state enterprises that existed under the FSLN, 289 were privatized by 1993, and all but eight by 1998.[15] The process had already begun, however, in the immediate aftermath of the 1990 election defeat. As the FSLN Vice President Sergio Ramírez described it in his memoirs:

> The fact is that Sandinismo could not go into opposition without material resources to draw upon, as this would have signified its annihilation. The FSLN needed assets, rents, and these could only be taken from the State, quickly, before the end of the three-month transition period. As a result there was a hurried and chaotic transfer of buildings, businesses, farms and stocks to third persons who were to keep them in custody until they could be transferred to the party.[16]

In the end, however, the Frente itself received almost nothing; but 'many individual fortunes were constituted through this process instead'. The episode is known as the *piñata*, after the decorated papier-mâché figure, generally filled with sweets, which blindfolded party guests strike with a stick until it breaks open—at which point a scramble ensues. The 1990 *piñata* effectively created the nucleus of an ex-Sandinista entrepreneurial grouping, with eminently capitalist interests.[17] These new elite factions have played a key role in Managua's latest phase of development.

---

[15] Mayorga, *Megacapitales de Nicaragua*, p. 59.

[16] Sergio Ramírez Mercado, *Adiós muchachos: Una memoria de la revolución sandinista*, Mexico 1999, p. 55, my translation.

[17] Since much of the property 're-expropriated' in the *piñata* had belonged to the Somoza clan or related Liberal cronies before their nationalization in 1980, this set in place a major clash of interests between returning Liberal *émigrés* and ex-Sandinistas, over which Chamorro attempted to adjudicate. Against the Liberals' greater leverage in the legislature, the Sandinistas retained the power to mobilize their base and could threaten mass riots and demonstrations. The conflict was finally resolved in the 'co-governance pact' of 1999 between the FSLN and Alemán's Liberals, in the context of an uptick in foreign investment flows—to maquiladora operations and tourist projects in particular—which raised spirits on both sides. Businesses associated with former FSLN leaders include financial service providers

Regime change saw the return of many wealthy Nicaraguans who had left Managua for the US in 1979. The 'Miami boys' and their frenetic conspicuous consumption 'transformed the Managua night: neon-lit bars and exclusive clubs, designer clothing, Nicaragua's first surf shop, one-hour photo processing, expensive cars cruising the scene'.[18] Global franchises such as McDonald's, Subway, Pizza Hut, the Hard Rock Café and TGI Friday arrived to cater to the new *émigré* arrivals. The defeat of the Sandinistas also brought an influx of Contras and their families to Managua, creating conditions for new social conflicts and spatial polarization. This was most evident in the emergence of new settlements with explicit political associations: *barrio* '3-80' in south-central Managua, for example, named after the *nom de guerre* of Enrique Bermúdez, former Lieutenant Colonel in Somoza's National Guard and commander of the Contras' Northern Front; or the 'Omar Torrijos' settlement in the east of the city. By the early 1990s Managua was widely nicknamed *la ciudad caótica*, 'the chaotic city'. Crime rates soared and youth gangs began to make their presence felt in the streets.[19]

Meanwhile Mayor Alemán—known as El Gordo ('Fatso')—undertook a systematic assault on the symbols of Sandinismo: the revolutionary murals were whitewashed or destroyed, the monument to FSLN martyr Carlos Fonseca blown up, countless streets renamed. Development aimed to 'beautify' the metropolis in order to make it more attractive to private investors: a huge illuminated fountain in front of the Metrocentro mall that spouted multi-coloured water; showpiece public works such as the construction of a new cathedral in the city centre or the restoration

---

(Fininsa, Interfin, Almacena); the Victoria de Julio and Agroinsa sugar refineries; the INPASA printers; media outlets (Canal 4 and Canal 10 television stations, Ya! and Sandino radio stations); and Agri-Corp, the biggest distributor of rice and flour in Nicaragua. The main players include former FSLN *comandante* and member of the National Directorate, Bayardo Arce Castaño, a major stakeholder in Agri-Corp and closely associated with real-estate company Inversiones Compostela, whose headquarters in Los Robles are on land obtained via the *piñata*; the Coronel Kautz brothers; Dionisio Marenco, current Mayor of Managua; the late Herty Lewites, Mayor from 2000–04; Samuel Santos López, FSLN Foreign Minister; and Francisco López Centeno, FSLN treasurer. See *La Prensa*, 13 February 2005 and 16 May 2005.

[18] David Whisnant, *Rascally Signs in Sacred Places: The Politics of Culture in Nicaragua*, Chapel Hill, NC 1995, p. 448.

[19] Police estimates suggest that the number of gang members in Managua increased five-fold during the 1990s: Policía Nacional de Nicaragua, *Boletín de la Actividad Delictiva* 32, 2001.

of the lakeside Malecón. Alemán's rough-and-ready style, combined with financial backing from his Miami-Cuban connections and an emergent clientelist network, provided the base for his progress to the presidency in 1996. Once elected, he built an opulent new presidential palace at a cost of $7 million, with an even larger illuminated fountain designed to 'send surges of water to varying heights in coordination with musical melodies'.[20]

The Alemán government's approach to urban infrastructure was epitomized in its break-up and privatization of the national electricity company, ENEL, starting from 1998. The sole bidder for its distribution network was the Spanish multinational Unión Fenosa, which immediately imposed price hikes on users ranging from 100 to 400 per cent, while contributing a minimum of investment to a grid that suffers daily power blackouts.[21] Although the population of Managua has grown exponentially, state-sponsored housing projects have been minimal since 1990: fewer than 8,000 housing units were built during the decade of Chamorro and Alemán governments.[22] Housing regulations developed under the FSLN were used for land clearances to favour developers: squatter families were evicted on this basis from the 22 de Enero settlement along the road to Masaya in 1999, before the Municipality of Managua re-categorized the land and invited tenders for it. In a country where 90 per cent of the economically active population earn less than $160 a month, luxurious gated communities and large hacienda-style homes for the new elite have proliferated in what was once Managua's

---

[20] 'Musical fountain for the President', *Envío in English*, 218 (1999). In office, Alemán rapidly became a byword for sleaze and corruption. State enterprises were sold to cronies at rock bottom prices, and a significant proportion of the $1 billion of international aid following Hurricane Mitch in 1998 was siphoned off. Alemán is estimated to have embezzled up to $100 million during his five years as President. In 2003 he was sentenced to 20 years' imprisonment for fraud and embezzlement; but in April 2007, FSLN and Liberal MPs proposed a law reducing the maximum penalty for money laundering to five years; if passed, it would enable Alemán to be granted parole as early as mid-2008.

[21] In early 2007 the Nicaraguan government attempted to fine Unión Fenosa $2.4 million and threatened to re-nationalize electricity distribution, but backtracked when it discovered it would be liable to pay the company $53 million in compensation.

[22] See Centre on Housing Rights and Evictions, 'Housing Rights in Nicaragua: Historical Complexities and Current Challenges', Geneva 2003, pp. 72–6.

bucolic peripheral zone. The Portal San Cayetano gated community in Las Colinas provides homes that offer 'a refined global neo-colonial mood' for $160,000 a throw.

Restoration economy

The same asymmetry has skewed the overhaul of Managua's legendarily bad road system. As late as 1997, potholes were a chronic driving hazard, carjackings frequent, traffic was chaotic, and there was no discernable logic to the city's byzantine road network. By 2000, the municipality had carried out a large-scale programme to resurface and widen the major arteries, and replaced traffic lights with roundabouts. These works were ostensibly intended to speed up traffic and reduce congestion. When considered on a map, however, a definite pattern emerges: the new roads predominantly connect locations associated with the lives of the urban elite, linking the newly re-modelled international airport to the Presidential palace, the 'Zona Rosa' of art galleries, embassies and fine restaurants to Las Colinas. Perhaps the most notorious is the 18 km stretch connecting the Southern Highway to the rural settlement of El Crucero, paved in 1999 at a cost of $700,000, in order to provide Alemán with easier access to his five haciendas. The living and working spaces of the wealthy—protected by high walls and private security—have been joined into a 'fortified network' by the new roads, which the elite can cruise at breakneck speeds in their expensive 4x4 cars, no longer impeded by potholes, crime or traffic lights. A whole layer of Managua's urban fabric has been deliberately 'ripped out' from the patchwork of the metropolis.

Predictably, there have also been massive tax exemptions for big real-estate developers, generally on the grounds that the monstrosities that they erect are 'tourist attractions': a $2.5 million tax break for the Pellas Group's 14-storey glass-and-metal office block, 'Edificio Pellas', for example. The interests at stake here are not simply those of Conservative and Liberal capital, however. The 'Incentives for the Tourist Industry' law that underwrote the tax exemptions was passed in June 1999 with the full support of Sandinista deputies who, under the leadership of Daniel Ortega, had entered into a 'co-governance pact' with Alemán shortly before. A leading figure in the debate was the founder member of the

FSLN, Tomás Borge, by this stage President of the Parliamentary Tourism Commission and owner of a hotel that stood to benefit. Arguably, what is emerging here is a Nicaraguan neo-oligarchy, split not by the old Conservative/Liberal rift but along a fault-line dividing a smaller national-bourgeois grouping (Liberal/Sandinista) from larger transnational capital (Liberal/Conservative). The former is composed of Liberals who did not leave the country during the 1980s, and whose economic interests are national in scope, including for example Alemán and his associates who benefited from the privatizations his government undertook, as well as Sandinistas who made fortunes through the *piñata*. The transnational capital bloc comprises Liberals who left Nicaragua during the revolution and successfully started businesses abroad, such as the Coen family, who founded the Airpak group in the US, a billion-dollar company that exclusively represents Western Union's financial services arm in Central America, as well as traditional Conservatives such as the powerful Pellas family.[23]

The major change in the city's productive economy in the 1990s was the introduction of Free Trade Zones. The first state-owned FTZ opened in Managua in 1992, and since then a further 24 privately owned ones have been established, mainly in and around the capital. The number of companies operating in them has grown from 5 in 1992 to 99 in 2006, while the number of workers employed has expanded from 1,000 in 1992 to 80,000 in 2006. A further 240,000 are employed indirectly, meaning that over 15 per cent of the Nicaraguan labour force is in employment related to FTZs. Export production through the FTZs

---

[23] The Pellas family owns the Banco de América Central financial conglomerate, the fifth largest financial group in the region with $3.1 billion in assets. They had backed the anti-Somoza alliance in 1979 but withdrew their support—and their capital—once the Sandinistas showed that they were serious about dissolving the National Guard and nationalizing Somocista property. Overall, though, this neo-oligarchy is very small. Francisco Mayorga, a former Nicaraguan Central Bank governor imprisoned under Alemán, claims that there are just 350 individual accounts in the Nicaraguan banking system with deposits amounting to more than $1 million, and that only twelve family groups own assets over $100 million: the Pellas Chamorro, Chamorro Chamorro, Lacayo Lacayo, Baltodano Cabrera, Ortiz Gurdián, Zamora Llanes, Coen Montealegre, Lacayo Gil, Fernández Holmann, Morales Carazo, González Holmann and Montealegre Lacayo. See Mayorga, *Megacapitales de Nicaragua*, pp. iii, 125.

has multiplied from $3 million in 1992 to $900 million in 2006, equivalent to 46 per cent of total Nicaraguan exports, and 87 per cent of manufactured exports. By far the largest activity is apparel assembly, with the companies involved mainly South Korean (24 per cent), US (23 per cent) and Taiwanese (17 per cent). Only 13 per cent are Nicaraguan. More significantly, however, some two-thirds of the private FTZs' infrastructure belongs to Nicaraguan entrepreneurs, who rent space within their compounds to foreign companies, while also receiving large tax exemptions.[24] Underpinning this is the planned busway system in northern Managua, which when completed will ferry up to 200,000 workers a day from the populous working-class Ciudad Sandino in the west of the city to the labour-hungry FTZs in the east, via several poor lakeside neighbourhoods whose populations are likely to provide secondary labour reservoirs.

In the barrio

The underlying dynamics of Managua's transformation can be traced in microcosm through the story of one poor neighbourhood in the southeast of the city. It was originally settled as an illegal squatter community in the early 1960s by migrants from the countryside, one of many such informal settlements that mushroomed at the time, although it rapidly became notorious in Managua for its extreme poverty. A long-time resident, Don Sergio, recalled:

> people had to do almost anything they could in order to make a living—wheel and deal, rob, scavenge on the streets and on the rubbish dumps, looking for anything that could be sold as scrap, recycled, or reused: old cans, bottles, paper, food, anything ... Even our houses were made of whatever we could scavenge—bits of wood, scrap metal, plastic, cardboard ... We were known as '*los Sobrevivientes*', because there was so much poverty here that you would surely die under normal circumstances. We didn't always

---

[24] They include not only major Nicaraguan conglomerates such as the Pellas Group but the Nicaraguan Army, which is also a major player in Managua's private real-estate development market, reportedly holding some $50m worth of shares in development companies. It is rumoured that several major Sandinista politicians, including Dionisio Marenco and Daniel Ortega, are also FTZ infrastructure owners. For a listing of FTZs, see www.laguiazf.org; on the Army, see Oliver Bodán, 'IPSM maneja $50 millones', *Confidencial*, 12–18 December 2004 and José Adán Silva, Luis Galeano and Mauricio Miranda, 'Ejército urbanizador', *El Nuevo Diario*, 10 November 2007.

eat, and there was lots of malnutrition, and many children and sometimes even adults died of disease and hunger.[25]

During the 1970s the *barrio* became a hotbed of resistance to the Somoza dictatorship. Several FSLN guerrilla cells were established in the neighbourhood, and it came under heavy attack from Somocista National Guard tanks and planes during the 1979 uprising. According to Don Sergio, there were few houses left standing. The *barrio* was singled out for improvement under the Sandinista redevelopment plan, and President Ortega came to announce the project:

> He told us how the Cubans had donated prefabricated houses to Nicaragua, and that because we were the poorest neighbourhood in all Managua, we had been chosen to be the pilot project for a new Sandinista approach to urban development. We were all to get houses, determined by lottery, and build them ourselves by means of Mutual Aid. And that's how it was, we all worked together, to build our *barrio*, everybody, the whole community. The houses, the roads, the alleyways, the electricity, the water, the sewage, everything was built through the efforts of the inhabitants of the *barrio*, and nobody else.

But Sandinista urban developments called for sustained follow-up and maintenance, both by local communities and the state. After initial enthusiasm and high participation levels, the former crumbled in the face of the growing economic crisis, while the government was increasingly preoccupied by the Contra war. The *barrio*'s newly built infrastructure—concrete drainage ditches, resurfaced roads, electricity provision—rapidly decayed. The situation deteriorated further under the Chamorro government, and by the mid-1990s, inhabitants frequently complained that things had 'come back full circle' to the poverty of the Somoza days. As Don Sergio put it:

> The houses are falling apart, the electricity's been cut off because nobody can afford it. Nobody cares about cleaning up the public areas of the *barrio*, nobody does anything for the upkeep of the neighbourhood. The streets are dark because none of the lights work anymore, the sewers are blocked, and the roads are pot-holed. Nobody does anything for the good of the community anymore, they only act for themselves, according to their self-interest. We're eating one another, as they say in the Bible.

---

[25] Interviewed by the author in 1996. Names have been changed.

Managua barrio, 1. *Top left, late 70s: wooden shacks, dirt roads; top right, 1981: Sandinista neighbourhood work brigade; bottom left, 1990s: barbed-wire fence; bottom right, 2000s: bricked windows and barbed wire.*

Crime and violence had become major preoccupations. People were manifestly afraid of leaving their homes and restricted themselves to a few fixed routes and destinations. Many of the windows were barred or even bricked up.[26]

By the early 2000s, although Nicaragua's macro-economic indicators had not improved much, there were clear signs of upgrading in some of the houses. In what had once been a relatively uniform neighbourhood of one-storey monochrome wooden houses, a significant proportion had been strikingly transformed: they were now bigger, rebuilt in brick and concrete, often painted in bright pastel colours, and in some cases even two stories high. Many were also now barricaded in an almost fort-like

---

[26] During the year I spent living in the barrio from 1996–97, the admonition, *cuidado las pandillas!* ('be careful of the gangs') became a familiar refrain, punctuating all comings and goings, to the extent that it almost had the equivalent verbal value of *hasta luego* ('see you later').

Managua barrio, 2. *Top left, 1990s: wood-built house; top right, 2000s: the same house, rebuilt through the remittance economy; bottom left: building a second storey, in a row of one-storey houses; bottom right: fortress.*

manner, with high walls, iron bars, and barbed wire. Inside, dirt floors, gas burners and second-hand furniture had been replaced by tiled kitchens, designer furnishings, wide-screen cable TV, mega-wattage sound systems, Nintendo game consoles and in one case a computer with broadband connection. In these better-off houses, the people now wore expensive watches, had the latest-model cellphones—in a neighbourhood where in the mid-1990s only a dozen households had land-lines—and bought imported processed foods from a supermarket, rather than ingredients from the local open-air market.

Most of these improvements were linked to specific processes of income generation, including labour migration—not only to the US, but increasingly to Guatemala and Costa Rica—the import of East Asian second-hand cars for use as taxis and, above all, drug trafficking. Cocaine dealing emerged in the neighbourhood around mid-1999, initially on a small scale but rapidly expanding into a three-tiered pyramidal economy. At the top was the *narco*, who brought the cocaine in from the Caribbean. The *narco* sold his goods wholesale to nine *púsheres* in the neighbourhood, who resold it in smaller quantities or converted it into crack, which they sold from their houses to a regular clientele of users and to nineteen *muleros*, the bottom layer of the pyramid, who in turn sold smaller doses of crack to all comers on the neighbourhood's streets. The potential rewards of being associated with the drugs trade were substantial: *muleros* made between $350 and $600 a month, for example, while *púsheres* would make over $1,000. In a neighbourhood where half the economically active population was unemployed, a further 25 per cent underemployed, and where those who did work earned a median monthly income of around $105, such sums were very significant. As a *mulero* called Kalia put it: 'it's the only thing worthwhile doing here in the *barrio*'.

A local *púsher* compared the drug-fuelled improvements to the Sandinista reconstruction of the neighbourhood in the early 1980s: 'Now it's been rebuilt like after the Revolution, except that instead of Sandinismo, it's the market that's been helping us.' Asked about the visible new levels of inequality, he replied: 'It's like the lottery that attributed the houses in the rebuilt *barrio*—some people got bigger and better located houses than others, but nobody complained because it was all random.' Yet drug trafficking has clearly created forms of inequality of a completely different order to those of the Sandinista years. The local power structure benefits those who can assert a relative monopoly over the use of violence: the *narco*, *púsheres* and *muleros* are all members or ex-members of local youth gangs, and have sought to precipitate a generalized state of fear in the *barrio* to ensure that the drug trade can operate unimpeded. A local woman commented on the deterioration of the gang members' ethos, from the greater sense of social solidarity in the mid-1990s:

> Before, you could trust the gang, but not anymore—they've become corrupted due to this drug crack. They threaten people from the neighbourhood now, rob them of whatever they have. They never did that before. They used to protect us, but now they don't care, they only look out for themselves, for their illegal business. People are scared—we live in terror here. You've got to be scared, or you're sure to be sorry.[27]

In the streets, gang members were now an intimidating presence, strutting about with guns and machetes menacingly displayed, and warning

---

[27] Interview with the author, 2002.

local inhabitants of what would follow if they denounced those involved in the drug trade. Levels of insecurity had risen sharply, as the gangs imposed a brutal and predatory form of order that seems unsustainable. One woman described the situation as 'living in a state of siege', a metaphor all the more chilling given that she lived through a real siege under the bombs and tanks of Somoza's National Guard during the insurrection of 1979.

Ortega's return

While Managua's *barrios* fracture into ganglands, elite factions continue to jostle for power in the new Nicaragua. Tensions sharpened between the Liberal–Conservatives, backed by Nicaragua's transnational finance firms, and the Sandinista–Liberal bloc, more closely tied to national agribusiness and *maquila* manufacturing interests, under the government of Enrique Bolaños (2002–07), who tilted strongly towards the former: poverty funds of $285 million were re-channelled to cover dubious bank losses. In the 2006 elections Daniel Ortega, once again FSLN presidential candidate, won a four-way contest against a divided opposition: despite heavy-handed efforts by Nicaraguan big business and the US ambassador, Alemán's Liberals and Bolaños's Conservatives refused to unite under a single banner. Viewed in the light of the evolving political economy of post-revolutionary Nicaragua, the result seems to represent a shift in fortunes towards the national-bourgeois bloc. Ortega's new cabinet reads like a veritable who's who of Sandinista businessmen: Bayardo Arce Castaño is the President's economic advisor; Arce's business partner Samuel Santos López is the new Minister of Foreign Affairs. Especially significant for Managua's urban development, the new Minister of Transport and Infrastructure is Fernando Martínez Espinoza, owner of one of Nicaragua's biggest construction companies; his Vice-Minister is Fernando Valle Dávila, head of the Nicaraguan Chamber of Construction. Furthermore, Ortega's Vice President is the Liberal Jaime Morals Carazo, founder of the Banco Nicaragüense (BANIC), co-founder with Alemán of the Constitutionalist Liberal Party (PLC), and advisor with the rank of cabinet minister during the latter's presidency.

In its first year in office, Ortega's administration has mixed anti-imperialist rhetoric and *rapprochement* with Chávez's Venezuela with trouble-free negotiations with the IMF, big business and improved relations with the US. Domestically, the focus seems to be on securing an economic settlement in which local businesses can derive sustainable, low-level profits from exclusive monopolies over certain protected sectors of the domestic market. There are few signs that this new Sandinista government is likely to inaugurate a more equitable phase of national development. A quarter of a century after the great earthquake, Managua now has a population of 1.2 million, over a fifth of the national total, and remains the focal point of all social, economic and political activity in the country. Symptomatically, however, despite its narco-*barrios* and brash new developments, its ruined city centre has still not been rebuilt.

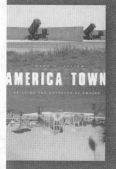

NEW TITLES FROM NORTON

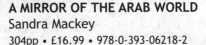

A MIRROR OF THE ARAB WORLD
Sandra Mackey
304pp • £16.99 • 978-0-393-06218-2

The recent history of Lebanon provides an insight into the many trials currently facing the larger Arab community. Sandra Mackey presents a view of the region, through the lens of this country.

DEFYING DIXIE
Glenda Elizabeth Gilmore
640pp • £25.00 • 978-0-393-06244-1

In a dramatic narrative, Gilmore traces the roots of the civil rights movement back to the 1920s, and recasts our understanding of the most important social movement in twentieth-century America.

THE ASSOCIATES
Richard Rayner
224 pp • £14.99 • 978-0-393-05913-7

Four Sacramento merchants become the force behind the US transcontinental railway 140 years ago. The story of 'The Associates' is one of ambition, greed and the making of a nation.

THE MODERN ELEMENT
Adam Kirsch
288 pp • £15.99 • 978-0-393-06271-7

A collection from one of today's most controversial and fearless critics, Kirsch scrutinizes the reputation of popular poets and admires the achievements of writers as different as Walcott, Milosz and Seidel.

www.wwnorton.co.uk

REVIEWS

Jerry F. Hough, *Changing Party Coalitions: The Mystery of the Red State–Blue State Alignment*
Agathon Press: New York 2006, $26.95, paperback
305 pp, 978 0 87586 407 5

Tom Mertes

AMERICAN DUOPOLY

Amid fears of recession at home and disillusion in Iraq, the collapse of Karl Rove's once-acclaimed electoral strategy—mobilizing a 'red-state' alliance of Southern whites, Midwest Evangelicals and security moms around God, guns and the War on Terror—prompts a longer-term look at the bloc-building tactics of American political elites. The merit of Jerry Hough's recent *Changing Party Coalitions* is the rigorously estranging eye it casts on these processes. A comparative political scientist at Duke University, Hough is best known for his work on the USSR, in which he set aside then dominant 'totalitarian' interpretations to focus on the actual institutional workings of the Soviet polity. Far from the monolithic dictatorship posited by the likes of Richard Pipes, Hough revealed a complex system of factions and countervailing tendencies; nor did he hesitate to draw parallels between the USSR's one-party system and the practices of the US duopoly, including elite management of faction-ridden parties and interest-group capture of policy-making. Here, he brings a similar independence of mind to his discussion of American electoral processes and the emergence of what he sees as the deliberately anti-democratic red-state/blue-state paradigm; in the process, many of the central episodes of a familiar narrative appear in a new light.

Since Walter Dean Burnham's *Critical Elections and the Mainsprings of American Politics* in 1970, a set of landmark presidential contests have been held to signal tectonic shifts of social and ideological support for the two hegemonic parties: 1800, 1828, 1860, 1896, 1932, 1968 and, latterly, 1980

REVIEW

and 2000. Hough recasts both the number of realignments and their meaning: he tends to see both parties as constructed from the top down, rather
than as substantiations of the people's will. Many features of the oligarchic
polity of the 18th century were preserved by the parties that emerged in
the 19th, who united to thwart the appearance of any populist alternative or
party of labour—an almost unique achievement in the New World. Hough's
account draws on intensive archival work to detail the processes by which the
two parties contrived to limit electoral participation, gerrymander constituencies and divide up the electoral spoils within the ferociously competitive
landscape of modern industrial America—greatly aided, although he does
not spell this out, by the first-past-the-post system. At stake, for both parties, has been the problem of mobilizing maximum electoral support for
policies that are not primarily conceived in the interests of the median voter.
According to Hough:

> both parties have structured their economic policy so as to try to maximize
> support in the upper class of the population—the 25 per cent of the population
> that makes above $75,000 a year in family income. Without any meaningful
> choice on economic questions, voters have been forced to choose between the
> parties on cultural issues alone.

In his view, the recent withdrawal of the two parties behind the winner-
takes-all ramparts of the red-state/blue-state division, leaving only a dozen
states genuinely competitive, represents a further diminution of the real
electorate, narrowing the already circumscribed space available for mean-
ingful political participation.

Changing Party Coalitions starts with the Democratic-Republican Party
constructed by Jefferson and Madison, tracing the logic of electoral cal-
culation as land- and slave-owning elites manoeuvred to shore up their
factions' votes within an Electoral College modelled on *ancien régime* lines.
The arithmetic had been sealed in the compromise at the Constitutional
Convention of 1787, which Hough describes as 'a velvet military coup d'état
against the Articles of Confederation, led by the man who controlled the
army'. George Washington presided over the Convention and used his two
former aides-de-camp—Alexander Hamilton from the North and James
Madison from the South—to put in place a mechanism that would restore
elite order and guarantee a unified state for external affairs, without interfering in domestic social hierarchies at local-state level. Parity for North and
South in the Senate and Electoral College was understood by the Framers
of the Constitution as providing the plantation-owners with a veto over
any legislation that would undermine the slave system; but broader alliances would be needed once political competition ensued. A distinctive
element of Hough's book is its grasp of the dynamic nature of ethnic and

religious allegiances within a fast-growing settler state. Early 18th-century colonists, he argues, still clung to the confessional loyalties of the English Civil War: the small towns and villages of Puritan New England were rife with suspicion towards the Episcopalian planters of Virginia. Between mid-century and the Revolution, however, a fresh wave of immigration was dominated by non-English Protestants—Presbyterian or Baptist Scots and Irish, Lutheran or Mennonite Germans and Dutch—who brought their own sets of loyalties and enmities. Many would settle in New York, Pennsylvania and Virginia.

In the first contested presidential election of 1796, Hough suggests, Jefferson and Madison calculated that the support they would need from the mid-Atlantic non-slave states to add to their Southern base could not be leveraged by appealing to small farmers of upper New York or Pennsylvania to ally with plantation-owners on the basis of their own perceived class or economic interests. Instead, the early Republicans appealed to the Puritan and anti-English sentiments of Scottish and Irish immigrants against the 'Anglo-Monarchical Tories'—i.e., Washington and the Federalists—and denounced Adams for wanting 'an aristocratical form of government'; as Hough notes, 'nothing was said about the truly aristocratic form of government in the South that Jefferson and Madison never tried to change.' Though initially unsuccessful, Jefferson's victory in 1800 formed the basis for the first party alignment. A decade later, Madison 'deliberately' provoked the War of 1812 against England on the same logic, to secure his own re-election, while the Federalists' opposition to the conflict terminally damaged their credibility as a national party.

In the 1830s Andrew Jackson, 'a Tennessee slave-owner of Ulster-Protestant stock', and Martin Van Buren, 'a Dutch-German New York' politician, initially aimed to build a new Democratic Party that would mobilize the burgeoning electorate on the same basis as Jefferson's Democratic-Republicans: that is, an alliance of Southern interests with Protestant Irish, Scots and Germans in the vote-rich mid-Atlantic states. Hough sees this coalition coming apart as the result of a third, mid-19th-century wave of immigration, from 1835–60, this time dominated by Catholic Irish and (to a lesser degree) Germans, fleeing famine, eviction and repression at home. They crowded the fast-expanding Northern cities and soon became fodder for, and then operators in, the clientelist Democratic machine, whereby jobs and favours were allocated in exchange for political loyalty. In Hough's revisionist view it was the tensions produced by the annexation of the vast Catholic territory of the south-west in the 1845 Mexican–American War that led to the breakdown of the mid-century Democrat–Whig alignment. When the Whigs, magnates and manufacturers failed to offer a refuge to Protestant workers alienated by the Irish-run lower ranks of the Democratic machine in the 1850s, they were swept away by the anti-Papist, anti-immigrant Know-Nothing Party in a revolt from below. The Republican Party, formed in 1854 as the first all-Northern party in the country's history, effectively rose to the task of consolidating 'the economic positions of the Whigs and, in a polite manner, the anti-Catholic themes of the Know-Nothings'—winning enough support among Northern German and Irish Protestants to take the presidency in 1860.

The Civil War itself is barely touched on in *Changing Party Coalitions*: the answer to the national question is assumed and the political–economic contradictions of the dual system go unexplored. In the view of this Sovietologist—shared, *mutatis mutandis*, by America's post-bellum leaders— the Civil War was an elite mistake, rendered irreversible by the destabilizing effects of 'premature democratization' in the rapidly industrializing repub- lic. Black disenfranchisement, the poll tax, literacy tests, the 'Australian ballot', Federal rather than state control over granting citizenship, and complex registration and residency requirements duly circumscribed the electoral politics of the post-Reconstruction era. Hough's focus in this period is mainly on the out-of-office Democrats and the reasons for their failure. The DP's control over the South was now uncontested; but to accumulate sufficient support to win the Electoral College, Democratic presidential can- didates had to focus their efforts either on the Midwest and Plains states, which would entail a campaign based on populist themes to appeal to hard-working farmers, or—less certain of success—on the Lutherans and Catholics of the Northern states. Viewed from the South, these choices pre- sented themselves as 'left fork'—orientation to the Plains—and 'right fork': the minority, mainly working-class Catholic vote in the East. With one excep- tion, the Democrats would opt for the right fork until the New Deal; populist appeals risked stirring up their own poor whites, while the Party machine could be guaranteed to deliver immigrant workers' votes in the big cities, whatever the platform. Hough quotes the editorial view of the *Charleston News and Courier* of December 1878:

> Our fixed opinion is that *the permanent interests of the South lie with the East rather than the West*. The aim of the South being to . . . avoid whatever is revo- lutionary in politics, sociology or finance, the South must go with the East.

As a result, DP candidates were 'consistently more conservative than their Republican counterparts', the only Democrat in the White House between 1860 and 1912, Grover Cleveland, distinguishing himself by his tight-money policies and by sending Federal troops to crush the Pullman railway work- ers' strike of 1894.

The sole Democratic candidate to attempt the left-fork strategy, promot- ing the 'free silver' bimetallist policy favoured by Midwest farmers over the big banks' gold standard, was William Jennings Bryan. The 1896 election and the Battle of the Standards is seen as pivotal in most accounts of America's party system—the moment when the big-money Republican campaign succeeded in winning an important section of Northern industrial workers over to the party of their bosses, aided by aggressively negative advertising. Karl Rove claimed to have styled Bush's 2000 campaign on the 1896 contest and looked to McKinley's strategist Mark Hanna as his intellectual forebear. But McKinley is barely mentioned in Hough's text, which sees no major break in the party coalitions until the New Deal. He focuses instead on Bryan's inexperience and underfunding, suggesting that the Democratic leadership knew they had no chance in 1896 after the deeply unpopular Cleveland Administration and had nominated Bryan solely to co-opt a growing Populist vote. In 1912, when the Democrats once again had a chance to win, they nominated the conservative governor of New Jersey, Woodrow Wilson. The son of a Scots-Irish Virginia Presbyterian, Wilson had all the requirements necessary to triumph over the already splintered Republicans (Taft versus 'Bull Moose' Roosevelt); the ticket was balanced by selection of Thomas Marshall from Indiana as his running mate. Wilson's Polkian invasions of Nicaragua, Mexico, Haiti and the Dominican Republic returned the Democrats firmly to imperial mode.

Hough rightly stresses the numerical weight of German-Americans—roughly equal to that of British-Americans—among the many 'European races' that constituted much of the US electorate during the first half of the 20th century. (He himself is of mixed German-American and British-American stock rooted in Carolina.) But at times Hough's tenacity on this question leads him to overstate its explanatory importance for the impact of US foreign policy on electoral outcomes, and vice versa, between 1912 and 1950. The need to shore up the German-American vote for the 1916 election was surely only one reason why Wilson did not enter the Great War as soon as the first trench was dug. As it was, he soon put Democratic congressmen under strain with his vituperative attacks on critics of his foreign policy as having 'alien sympathies'. Wilson's 1902 *History of the American People*, as Hough drily notes, had favourably compared the 'sturdy stocks of the north of Europe' to more recent arrivals, describing the Ellis Island immigrants as 'men of the lowest class from the south of Italy and men of the meaner sort out of Hungary and Poland', as these countries 'disburdened themselves of the more sordid and hapless elements of their population.' But his 1915 State of the Union address was targeted at the many German-American opponents of the War: US citizens 'born under other flags but welcomed under our generous naturalization laws . . . who have poured the poison of disloyalty into the very arteries of our national life'—'such creatures of passion, disloyalty and anarchy must be crushed out.' Wilson narrowly won the 1916 election but lost the German-Irish states of Illinois, New York, New Jersey and Indiana that he had carried in 1912. (In contrast, he picked up California after advocating the withdrawal of property-holding rights from Japanese-Americans.) Senators from states with large Irish and German-American populations refused to ratify the punitive Treaty of Versailles, and in the 1920 elections the Democrats lost miserably, having fielded anti-immigrant candidates. But Hough is wrong to say that when Wilson 'brought the war home' after the termination of hostilities with the Palmer Raids on radical immigrants, the targets were Germans; the assaults were directed almost entirely against Russians.

The Democrats returned to the Oval Office with the election of Roosevelt in 1932, which—here Hough agrees with the received wisdom—marked another major partisan realignment. In Hough's eyes, Roosevelt had effectively opted for a 'left-fork' strategy based on the South and West, to harvest the voters who had supported the 'collectivist' candidacy of Robert LaFollette in 1924, in place of the orientation to the urban Northeast of the belle-époque Progressives; yet the Keynesian stabilization policies that he then pursued had not been articulated in the 1932 campaign. Hough points out that many New Deal policies were directed at rural areas: electrification, increase in farm prices, the large-scale dam projects; equally, many benefited the South. As a Sovietologist, he is well placed to deflate excessive claims for Roosevelt's radicalism, charging that few commentators today are prepared to acknowledge 'how cautious the New Deal was in comparative terms, nor how far we have come from it since.' Once Roosevelt had secured a landslide re-election and forced the Supreme Court to back down, he did little to deepen the reforms. But the New Deal party alignment persisted: the Democrats stood as the party of the working class, new immigrants and Northern blacks, as well as the South; while the Republicans were relegated to a pan-Protestant Northern and Western strategy.

World War Two again divided German- and British-Americans. After Pearl Harbor, Roosevelt tried to tread more carefully than Wilson had done, and made sure that German-Americans—Dwight Eisenhower, Chester Nimitz, Carl Spaatz—were appointed to top military posts to lead the assault on the Axis powers. The 7,000 German-Americans arrested in 1942 as people of 'Foreign Enemy Ancestry' were treated very differently to the vast numbers of Japanese-Americans thrown into internment camps; yet FDR still lost votes from German-American precincts. The start of the Cold War and the division of Germany created further tensions. In 1949 a majority of senators in the band of eleven states from Pennsylvania to Nevada voted against ratification of the NATO treaty, institutionalizing Germany's partition. In general, Hough argues, Republican Administrations during the Cold War were more open to the détente policies favoured by the German-American component of their constituency, while Democratic presidents were more aggressively anti-Communist: Truman in Korea, Kennedy planting missiles in Turkey, invading Cuba and sending US troops to Vietnam, while Nixon negotiated with Mao and Reagan with Gorbachev. He admits that the picture is blurred, however, by the fact that each side compensates by proclaiming an ideological stance that is the opposite of its actions.

Conventional wisdom usually sets the end of the New Deal coalition with Reagan's election in 1980, or with Carter's anti-inflation policy in 1979. But in the most radical and original section of his argument, Hough makes a strong case for placing the beginning of the end much earlier, with JFK. In his acceptance speech at the 1960 Democratic Convention, Kennedy defined himself not as a New Dealer but as a New Democrat and signalled that 'the old ways will not do'. Like Adlai Stevenson, another business-friendly Democrat, Kennedy needed to select a New Deal Southerner to balance the ticket. In office, his economic policy of balanced budgets and tax cuts for the rich was 'less liberal than Richard Nixon's', and he was 'quite cautious, perhaps even conservative, on cultural issues such as civil liberties and civil rights'. In the foreign-policy sphere, Hough suggests that 'those who think that [Kennedy] would have avoided Johnson's deepening engagement in Vietnam are taking a most improbable leap of faith. A more realistic question is whether he would have acted more boldly in threatening to send troops to overthrow the regime in Hanoi.' If it had not been for the 'accidental' presidency of Lyndon B. Johnson, he argues, the New Deal would have been a thing of the past.

Instead LBJ, the first Confederate president for 120 years, introduced a raft of radical domestic policies that would finally put an end to the autonomy of the South and, at the same time, open it to political competition. It also marked the end of the 'European races', now officially recast as 'whites'. The entry of the GOP into the South famously signals the next stage in party realignments. But Hough makes a plausible case for the fluke of the Johnson Administration obscuring the real evolution of Democratic strategy, which was otherwise moving, from Kennedy onwards, in the direction of a 'blue-state' approach, founded on appeals to the economic interests of better-off suburban voters in the North. Hough describes this as a return to the Progressive tradition of Wilson and a distinct shift to the right. McGovern's unsuccessful bid in 1972 represented the next stage in the process, according to this account. Although his campaign was radical on economic and anti-war issues, its ultimate effect was to help boost through Democratic Party ranks a layer of 1960s activists who would become the main trend-setters for the blue-state orientation once they entered Congress in 1974. Gary Hart is offered as the prototype of these upwardly mobile baby-boomers, who combined the right-wing economic policies and cultural liberalism characteristic of the New Democrats under Clinton. Ironically, however, the strategy of the next Democratic president, Jimmy Carter (1976–80), would prefigure something closer to Rove and Bush. Carter was the first occupant of the Oval Office to declare himself a born-again Christian (although Hough detects a whiff of Elmer Gantry). He aimed to win back the South from George Wallace by mobilizing the Evangelicals, while at the same time implementing an aggressively right-wing foreign and economic policy: supporting Somoza and the Shah, funding the Islamists in Afghanistan; cutting social spending at home and implementing the interest hike of the 'Volcker shock'. But Carter antagonized the Catholic component of his coalition, and his spending cuts alienated working-class voters who still embraced the ideology of the New Deal.

By comparison to the blue-state turn of the Democrats, the Republicans' move to a red-state strategy started later and was more defensive, according to Hough. Nixon aimed to maintain the Northern-based liberal Republican coalition, while courting the South with attacks on 'cultural radicals'. At the same time, the Evangelical churches were coming to play a more significant electoral role as genuine party competition in the South intensified. Desegregation had led to a rash of white Evangelical schools, which also increased their social leverage. For much of the postwar period they were 'a swing group at the presidential level', but they were to switch definitively to the Republican camp with Reagan—pushed, according to Hough, by the Democrats' 'move to the cultural left and economic right in the 1970s and 1980s'. Reagan is portrayed here as a rhetorician rather than an ideologue: though he spoke to conservatives' values, he implemented little of their policy agenda. Hough thinks Reagan inveighed against the Evil Empire mainly to 'relieve American anxieties about accepting compromise with the Soviet Union.' (The withdrawal of Marines from Lebanon is taken as another sign of Reagan's moderation; his continuation of Carter's policies in Honduras, Nicaragua and El Salvador goes unmentioned.) Electorally, his major role was to draw in male voters, in flight from the Democrats' feminist-oriented cultural liberalism, and shore up Evangelical support in the South. By 1984, the Civil War had been inverted: 'Reagan won the former states of the Confederacy and the border states of Kentucky, Missouri and Oklahoma by a 7.4 million vote majority.' Far from pursuing a red-state strategy, however, the Reagan Republicans aimed to compete country-wide.

The Democrats were faced once again with a left-fork or right-fork choice: to fight for middle America on an economically radical, if culturally moderate, line; or to withdraw from competition and focus on the Northern suburbs, as cultural liberals but economic conservatives. The decision was sealed by the capture of the party machine by the now 'affluent liberal' baby-boom activists and feminists, who picked up the Wilsonian baton of Adlai Stevenson and JFK. The anti-New-Deal direction was hardened by the

REVIEW

Democratic Leadership Council, formed in 1985, and embodied in Clinton: a presidential candidate from the South whose message was 'directed at the relatively well-to-do of the large industrial states'. Hough dismisses any suggestion that Clinton did not know what he was doing in the first two years of his administration: on the contrary, the team of economic super-hawks (Rubin, Summers) and strong cultural message (gays in the military) were entirely calculated, as was the unimplementable health-care pro-gramme entrusted to his wife and the decorative 'diversity' (labour, women, blacks) of the lower ranks. Clinton 'deliberately seems to have encouraged a misleading chaos to obscure a suburban strategy already chosen that he knew would be highly frustrating to many supporters and voters'. While the Democrats needed to maintain their traditional base among blacks, the working class and the unions, they had no intention of funding their prom-ises. Once in office, Clinton reportedly told his economic team, 'We're all Eisenhower Republicans—we stand for lower deficits and free trade and the bond markets'.

By the early 1990s, then, lower- and middle-income voters were left 'with no perceived economic choice in either party'. The scale of their disenchant-ment is measured here in the 19.7 million votes for Ross Perot in 1992, which Hough interprets as a welling up of dissatisfaction, among white males above all, at the impending passage of NAFTA—a proxy for globali-zation, outsourcing of jobs and generic threats to national pride. Neither Clinton nor Dole, in 1996, sought to address or co-opt the concerns that had made Perot's third-party candidacy so successful. On the contrary, Clinton's pollster Mark Penn announced to the Cabinet that the President's re-election signalled 'the end of the old Democratic coalition of blacks, the elderly, and the downscale. It marks the emergence of a new coalition of women, Latinos and especially suburban married couples.' Meanwhile Al Gore's speech-writer Kenneth Baer applauded the 'profound change' that had brought a Democratic president who championed 'the reinvention of government, welfare reform, fiscal restraint, free trade and an internationalist foreign pol-icy'. Under Clinton, Hough argues, the 'Democrats had basically returned to the [economic policies] of Grover Cleveland'.

The 2000 election was the first to show a clear 'red/blue' division: the richer, more urban and populous Northern and Pacific states voting for Gore, the poorer Midwest, plus the Sunbelt and the South, going for Bush. The popular vote was almost equally divided and the turnout was only 51 per cent of those of voting age. Hough suggests that it was probably Gore's choice of running-mate that lost him the election: while Joe Lieberman did well in eastern Florida, he may have cost Gore votes among Midwestern German-American retirees on the west side of the state. Had Gore bal-anced his ticket with Dick Gephardt, 'a German-American Protestant from

Missouri who favoured a New Deal strategy', he might have won both there and in West Virginia. By choosing the hawkish Lieberman, 'from a coastal state and with very close ties to the Connecticut insurance industry', the DP were effectively withdrawing from the competition in what would now become the red states.

Similarly, the Republicans took the decision to concede the coastal states and the industrial north. Hough suggests that, looking ahead from 1998, GOP strategists had seen 2000 as a losing year: the economy was booming and the Vice President was a well-connected contender. The electoral trend had marked a fall-off in Republican votes from Reagan's high of 55 million in 1984 to just over 39 million in 1992 and 1996, whereas the Democrats had steadily risen from 38 million to over 47 million in the same period. The party's high-level Brock Commission Report published in May 2000 suggested that the Republicans were facing an unacceptably large loss of Northern suburban voters. Produced after Bush's nomination, and based on the implicit assumption of a third straight loss, the Brock Commission called for reforms to the party's nomination procedure. The 'front-loaded' system, privileging the least populous states, had produced two candidates from Texas and one from Kansas. The Commission wanted a bigger role for the urban North; a Republican red-state strategy was assumed to have a limited future.

Faced with this unpromising situation, Rove chose to focus on intensive mobilization of the 239 Electoral College votes of the Southern, Prairie and Mountain states, with hopes of 33 more from Indiana and Ohio; Bush's running-mate Dick Cheney was from Wyoming. The aim was to bring out the disaffected Ross Perot vote through a strong emphasis on cultural conservatism. Hough suggests that Bush had not said much about religion before 1999: as with Carter, Jesus came late to his political life, along with brush-clearing on the ranch and other homespun themes. Again, Hough sees a strong Perot factor in Bush's hawkish national-security appointments—in 1992 Perot had excoriated Bush Senior's conduct of the Gulf War—and in his anti-foreigner rhetoric on Kyoto and the ABM Treaty. In 2004, Bush even adopted as his slogan the title of Perot's 1992 campaign book, *United We Stand*. The Democrats were unlikely to win the 2004 election; but here too, Kerry repeated the errors of Gore and failed to engage with economic issues, helping Bush to make inroads even into the blue states with tax cuts and post-9.11 nationalist bluster.

After taking readers as far as the 2004 election, *Changing Party Coalitions* ends with a call for two rather minor reforms. First, popular presidential elections, thus doing away with the Electoral College machinery which can no longer have 'any positive role' now that North and South are effectively homogenized; second, a single national primary for each party, both to reduce the role of party activists and to reverse the 'front-loading' of the nomination process. The first would certainly be positive, though the second risks handing still more power to the party bosses. Hough's main concern, however, is to ensure the stability of US political institutions and the continuation of the duopoly. 'Let us hope', he writes, 'that one or both parties find a way to represent the economic interests of the middle income in a sustainable way. Let us hope a major third party is not necessary.' The framework of his analysis could, however, be used to argue for the opposite—a multi-party system based on different classes, value-interested segments of the population and disparate regions.

Hough argues that the large-scale disenfranchisement effected by the red/blue alignment—connived at by both parties, so that neither need offer an economic policy that would answer to the interests of the great mass of median voters—is unsustainable. He fears that unbalanced deficits, unprecedented inequality and high personal indebtedness could make for serious instability in the event of a major shock. In the longer term, the undermining of the US polity by the disappearance of its structuring matrices—the North–South question, and the compensatory effect of the many 'European races'—has yet to be seriously addressed. Unstated, but strongly implied in his argument, is the need for a more equitable, probably protectionist, economic policy; nor does he ever spell out whether he would also support tougher limits on immigration. A new edition of *Changing Party Coalitions* would surely point out that neither question will be up for debate in the 2008 election.

An important feature of Hough's account is the generational remaking, or refabrication, of ethnic allegiances. Anglicans and Puritans were redefined—and redefined themselves—as English, in face of a new wave of Irish and German immigrants; Ulstermen and Lutherans became Protestants with the arrival of the mainly Catholic wave of Irish and Germans in the mid-19th century. The latter differentiated themselves from the Ellis Island immigrants from the 1890s on: *mezzogiorno* farmworkers and East European Jews. In the 1960s came the fabrication of the 'European races' of English-, German-, Irish-, Jewish- and Italian-Americans into the 'white' race, not least by immigration and civil-rights legislation. This amounted, as Hough points out, to a *de facto* acceptance of the South's formulation of 'race' as a black–white dichotomy. (On this question, it is strange that in such a well-referenced work there is no mention of Alexander Saxton's *The Rise and Fall of the White Republic*.) Hough estimates that today, 'blacks are where the Irish were in 1910, or Italians, Jews and Poles in 1950—not ideal, but a long way from the original prejudices and discrimination'.

This seems optimistic. According to 2006 US Government data, the new-fabricated 'whites'—198 million of a total of just under 300 million—earned on average $52,000 a year, compared to a national median of $48,000, and had an unemployment rate of 4 per cent, compared to a national average of 4.6 per cent. 'Hispanic-Latinos', the largest 'minority' at 43 million, earned $38,000 on average, with an unemployment rate of 5.3 per cent. 'Asians', another fabricated quantity, numbered 14 million, earned an average $64,000, and had a 3 per cent unemployment rate. 'Black' Americans, many of whom may trace their US ancestry to the time of the Founding Fathers or before, constituted 40 million, earned an average $32,000, and suffered an unemployment rate of 9 per cent. Yet it would be in line with Hough's analysis if both 'black' and 'white' Americans were to be refabricated, or refabricate themselves, as 'Christians' or the yet-more artificial 'Judeo-Christians', in the context of a new generation of mainly Muslim Subcontinental immigrants and an international situation not incomparable to that of Wilson's; or as 'English-speakers', in face of a much larger number of 'Latino-Hispanic-Americans'. The huge wave of protests in Spring 2006 against the iniquitous treatment of the mass immigrant population has highlighted the possibility that the circle cannot be squared within the current system.

Changing Party Coalitions offers a ruggedly idiosyncratic take on the American political system, deeply researched and widely read. Hough has been well served by his publisher, Agathon Press: footnotes are helpfully placed at the bottom of each page and the list of archives alone should make it essential reading for serious students of the country's political history. That said, the book also suffers from the weaknesses of its strengths. There is no detailed treatment of the parties' corporate funding, which is the real determinant of their economic policies. The author more than overstates his case in suggesting that domestic electoral concerns largely motivate, rather than inflect, America's foreign policy, and there is no attempt to correlate the different relationships between domestic groups and their homeland lobbies. Programmatically, no serious discussion of US electoral reform can avoid the question of the winner-takes-all system and the possibilities of more proportional forms of representation.

A more fundamental analytical problem is that Hough's institutionalist approach, in which party elites organize factions on a sectoral and geographical basis, ignores any dynamic from below. His reliance on ethnicity and religion as explanatory determinants tends to occlude class from his account of the US political system. Yet this was a major factor in several of the realignments he discusses. The attempt by 19th-century Republicans to develop a national manufacturing and infrastructure base behind high tariff barriers entailed an ongoing battle with agricultural-commodity producers in the South and West, organized through the Democrats, who wanted low tariffs. These positions broadly overlapped with geographic, confessional and ethnic divisions for much of the century, but by its end the economic and political landscape had been transformed, with agriculture secondary to the industrial sector. In the 1896 election much of skilled labour, including many German and Irish workers, formerly part of the Democrat coalition, voted for 'solid money' and McKinley. Thereafter the Democrats had to remodel their coalition according to the new realities of an urban industrial society.

Much more starkly, Roosevelt's leftward shift in 1932 was not simply a matter of seizing the electoral opportunities generated by the Great Depression, but also a response to a significant challenge from below. The pressures on capital from a hungry and radicalized working class that led to the New Deal are absent from Hough's analysis. Nor is there any real explanation for the North's abrogation of Southern autonomy in the 1960s, the major turning point in his account, or of the changing shape of the American economy since then: the industrializing South, the expansion of the Sunbelt suburbs, decline of the rustbelt and financialized self-gratification of the coastal elites. The internal tensions resulting from the increasing integration of the US with the world economy are gestured towards rather than evaluated. Hough notes the unravelling of the New Deal and the rightward movement of both parties in economic policy, but leaves out the social, economic and ideological transformations of which these are symptoms, and the dramatic alteration in the balance of forces in favour of capital that has accompanied them. Against this backdrop, Hough's hope that the parties will henceforth 'represent the economic interests' of the median mass of voters seems like whistling in the wind. Certainly, neither of the Democratic contenders in 2008 has plans to do so.

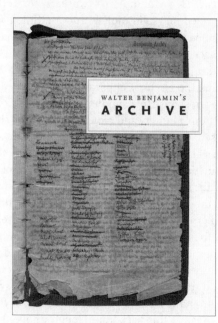

Franco Moretti, ed., *The Novel, Volume 1: History, Geography and Culture*
Princeton University Press: Princeton NJ 2006, $35, paperback
916 pp, 978 0 691 12718 7

Franco Moretti, ed., *The Novel, Volume 2: Forms and Themes*
Princeton University Press: Princeton NJ 2006, $35, paperback
950 pp, 978 0 691 13473 4

JOHN FROW

THINKING THE NOVEL

Along with the movie and the advertisement, the novel is the central aesthetic form of our time. Yet it is clear that, despite our association of the
novel with modernity, narrative forms looking remarkably like the modern novel arise in periods as diverse as Hellenistic antiquity and medieval
France, and can be found in quite other civilizations, notably China. It is
tempting to describe the novel as a collection of very disparate genres (as an
influential essay by Gustavo Pérez Firmat once put it) rather than a singular
and coherent form. Alternatively, we can think, as Mikhail Bakhtin does, of a
series of parallel histories working through successive transformations and
incorporating a range of other genres in the shaping of the loosely related
forms that we think of as making up the contemporary novel.

The two volumes of *The Novel* (distilled from the five volumes of the
prior Italian collection, *Il Romanzo*) contribute substantially to raising and
theorizing these questions. You could say, schematically, that there are
two main lines of filiation in twentieth-century novel theory, one running
from Georg Lukács's *Theory of the Novel* (1917), the other from the work
of Bakhtin. In Lukács's great essay an essentializing account of genre is
mapped onto an essentializing story about history, such that the novel's
historico-philosophical force is seen to lie in the coincidence of its structural categories with those of the modern world. Deeply time-bound, the
novel is defined by the negative shape of its central categories: its fall from

epic totality to 'modern' fragmentation, its thematization of the lack of fit between the problematic individual and the dead or demonic world of social convention, the principle of irony which seeks to correct the world's lack of immanent meaning, and a temporality which is at once the dead weight of routine, an order of memory, and the impossible promise of a future transcendence. Bakhtin's work, by contrast, is concerned less with the correspondence of social with literary forms than with the transformative work of novelistic discourse on the discourses that carry the social.

This collection is, by and large, much more interested in the Lukácsian problematic of the relation between morphology and social forms. In his brief foreword to Volume One, Franco Moretti writes that 'the novel is always commodity and artwork at once: a major economic investment and an ambitious aesthetic form . . . Don't be surprised, then, if an epistemological analysis of "fiction" slides into a discussion of credit and paper money or if a statistical study of the Japanese book market becomes a reflection on narrative morphology'. There's a version of this concern in Andrew Plaks's essay on the emergence of the Chinese novel, when he writes that

> such long-range trends as population shifts to the great cities of the Yangtze Delta region and the rise of urban culture, the conversion to a silver-based money economy, commercialization, commodification, incipient industrialization—even overseas colonization, to name just the most striking factors, seem not entirely unrelated to the appearance of a new form of prose literature so well suited to questioning the values of the old order.

These arguments have to do with underlying conditions, but Plaks then moves to pose the question in terms of the formal categories organizing this new genre: in the period of the classic Chinese novel the 'paradigmatic Confucian act of self-cultivation' shifts 'from the moral integrity of the autonomous individual acting within the web of human relations (in Chinese, the physical person: *shen*) to the ideal of integral wholeness at the core of the inner self, expressed with the term *xin* ("heart" or "mind")'.

Yet questions of structural correspondence can all too easily become reliant on a notion of the homogeneity or homology of different dimensions of the social, and this is often particularly a problem with understandings of modernity that collapse quite divergent processes into a singular whole. John Brenkman's argument that 'the novel's inner form belongs to the nihilism of modernity' is one version of this conflation; Moretti's essay 'Serious Century', on the novel's relation to private life, is another. Here Moretti relates Weber's analysis of the growing regularity, methodicalness and standardization of private life to the role of narrative 'fillers', story points which convey the routines of daily life rather than the events which break it. 'Fillers' in the novel offer a kind of narrative pleasure compatible with the new regularity of bourgeois life and with the underlying category of rationalization. The latter is described as 'a process that begins in the economy and in the administration, but eventually pervades the sphere of free time, private life, entertainment, feelings . . . Fillers are an attempt at *rationalizing the novelistic universe*: turning it into a world of few surprises, fewer adventures, and no miracles at all', and through them 'the logic of rationalization pervades *the very rhythm and form of the novel*'.

Thinking about the novel in this way, in terms of what its structures have in common with the structure of the world, tends to yield a kind of socio-thematics of modernity. Both Thomas Pavel and (with considerably more originality) Nancy Armstrong develop thematic accounts of the Lukácsian figure of the problematic individual and his or her lack of fit with the social order. Hans Gumbrecht and Margaret Cohen elaborate the novelistic figures (in Bakhtinian terms, the chronotope) of the road and the sea, respectively. Philip Fisher, in his essay 'Torn Space', follows Simmel, Kracauer and Benjamin in constructing a thematics of the experience of space in modernity around the general categories of stimulus and shock and the more specific historical development of the department store, of open-plan bourgeois interiors, and of new communications technologies such as the telephone, the radio and television; Joyce's *Ulysses* is then read, effectively, as a description of this new structure of experience. This is to say that thematic modes of reading can all too readily slip into accounts of a represented real, as though that real were independent of the generic and linguistic forms of its representation. At the same time, positing too direct a connection between novel and world can simplify the complex specificities of each. Invoking Braudel's notion of the 'plurality of social times', Jonathan Zwicker, in 'The Long Nineteenth Century of the Japanese Novel', complains that 'when the chronologies of such different histories as those of political institutions, literary form, and cultural practice coincide as well as they do in the conventional histories of nineteenth-century Japan, it is often because something has been overlooked. Dazzled by the event, we have somehow lost track of the different calibrations of social life'.

One of the most promising alternatives to conventional literary history in recent years has been the rise of book history and of the statistical methodologies it has tended to employ. Franco Moretti has been a prominent advocate of shifting literary history away from its attention to exceptional moments—the tiny minority of texts that constitute events within the literary series—to a study of its routine configurations, using large masses of data to chart patterns of production, circulation and consumption and thereby dispensing both with the individual text and its readings, and with the ideological functions of the proper name. As Jonathan Zwicker puts it in

a second contribution, 'Japan 1850–1900', one of the book's more thought-
ful methodological reflections:

> by treating books as *things*, quantitative data allows access to a comparative
> dimension of literary history that is difficult when anecdote remains the pri-
> mary mode of investigation. There is no doubt that numbers flatten out the
> peculiarities and individuality of their objects, but this is also part of their value,
> they 'simplify the better to come to grips with their subject' [Braudel] and so
> make accessible—through patterns and series—solutions to problems that
> are virtually inaccessible through the methods of traditional literary history.

In accordance with this challenge the collection gives some prominence
to historical accounts of particular markets and, more generally, of the material conditions of novelistic representation. In particular, a section of Volume
One develops a series of statistical profiles of the market for novels in Britain,
the United States, Italy, Spain, India, Japan and Nigeria over varying time
frames from the mid-eighteenth century to the present. John Austin's essay
on the United States between 1780 and 1850 draws a conclusion which,
mutatis mutandis, exemplifies those drawn by many of these essays:

> the failure of the American novel to triumph over its British competi-
> tor and to establish cultural hegemony over the course of the nineteenth
> century is striking.

> And, one should emphasize, markedly at odds with most accounts of
> 'American' literature. And herein resides the usefulness of quantitative analy-
> sis; it holds forth the promise of producing some new facts, of bringing
> into focus new genres (like the tale and compilation) and new formations
> in the literary field (the competition between American and British novels).
> Most important, such data enriches and complicates conventional narrative
> accounts of national (international?) literatures.

Elsewhere, Daniel Couégnas's essay on popular narrative looks at the origins of the novel in *colportage* texts (chapbooks) sold by peddlers, and at the
industrial and commercial techniques underlying the English Gothic novel
and the French *roman-feuilleton*. Zwicker's two essays on the Japanese novel
seek to map the play of continuities and discontinuities in the nineteenth-
century circulation in Japan of indigenous and translated texts. Many other
essays build elements of economic, demographic or institutional analysis
into their treatment of the life of the novel in particular areas.

Yet such analysis is, in the long run, only useful to the extent that it can
open up for us something of the way readers engaged with the novel: how it
helped shape their world of sense and emotion, how it spoke to them, how
they interpreted and put to use the words they consumed. None of this is
simply given in the data, and indeed the shift from patterns of production,

circulation and consumption to an understanding of readings and uses is fraught with difficulty. Roger Chartier puts it (as usual) neatly in a passage from his *Forms and Meanings* (1995) quoted by Zwicker, on the scarcity and difficulty of evidence for a history of practices of reading. Representations of reading, Chartier writes,

> never involve immediate and transparent relations with the practices they describe. All are lodged in the specific modes of their production, the interests and intentions that produced them, the genres in which they were inscribed, and the audiences at which they were aimed. To reconstruct the conventions that governed literate representations of [reading], therefore, we must decipher the strong but subtle bond that ties these representations to the social practices that are their object.

Readings happen inside people's heads; to gain access to them we must rely on secondary manifestations, most of which consist of one or another form of self-report (from marginalia or private letters to public reviews and survey responses) and all of which are dependent upon translation of the micro-processes of reading into a particular language. That language is not a faithful reproduction of psychological processes but a conventional articulation of them, however much it may in turn shape those processes: any self-report of reading necessarily employs a time-bound critical vocabulary, and this introduces a certain displacement into our analysis of reading. Where we expect to find the idiosyncrasy of a personal encounter with the text, we find rather the conventions of a historically and culturally specific regime. We can, as an alternative to studying individual readings, choose to study *readerships*, the correlation between a demographic formation and particular modes of encounter with texts. But in the forms that such analysis usually takes—particularly the audience research that is a central component of the study of the mass media—readerships become autonomous of texts, ready-formed independent variables which are not themselves shaped by the textual encounter. None of the essays in this collection overcomes this central methodological problem.

A further difficulty raised by quantitative analysis has to do with the constitution of its units of analysis. Zwicker sets up a useful contrast between two ways of theorizing a historical series: on the one hand, historians of a nominalist bent like Skinner or Pocock would argue that in tracing the history of concepts such as the state (or, by analogy, 'the novel') it is only ever possible to construct a history of the range of uses of those terms. On the other hand, however, Zwicker invokes Koselleck's argument for a history of structures that would treat terms such as 'the novel' as structurally real: instead of a series of more or less discrete semantic events, taking 'the novel' (or 'the state') as a real phenomenon underlying its historically and culturally various manifestations allows one to elaborate common structures across very different kinds of society.

Such an approach repeats the essentialism that informs both Lukács's and Bakhtin's conception of the novel, and it continues to depend upon the initial assumption of generic unity. It repeats, too, the core methodological move Moretti makes in *Graphs, Maps, Trees* (2005), of taking genres or forms as given and then deriving structures from large data sets based on them in such a way that literary history can be conceived as an objective account of patterns and trends. Moretti does in fact recognize that quantitative research 'provides a type of data which is ideally independent of interpretations . . . and that is of course also its limit: it provides *data*, not interpretation'. Thus he argues, correctly, that 'a formal concept is usually what makes quantification possible in the first place: since a series must be composed of homogeneous objects, a morphological category is needed—"novel", "anti-Jacobin novel", "comedy", etc.—to establish such homogeneity'. But he proceeds nevertheless to ignore the crucial point that these morphological categories he takes as his base units are not pre-given but are constituted in an interpretive encounter and by means of an interpretive decision.

Too many of the essays in this collection still perform a very old-fashioned kind of literary history in which that moment of interpretive constitution of the categories of analysis is disregarded; too much of this work (reflecting larger disciplinary assumptions) is positivist history uninformed by a close interpretive engagement with texts. Nathalie Ferrand's discussion of a database of novelistic topoi is the parodic extreme here, but many of the national histories, too, while factually informative, are records of events rather than encounters with textual complexity. The historicist turn in literary studies has, I think, for all its real achievements in rethinking literary texts within broader social and cultural frameworks, often tended to reinforce such a reduction of complexity and a relative lack of interest in the force of formal categories.

A more satisfying form of historicism is at work, however, in a number of essays that investigate the cultural circumstances in which the novel emerges and flourishes. Some of the most interesting analyses have to do with the changing status of the category of fictionality. Jack Goody's opening essay, 'From Oral to Written: An Anthropological Breakthrough in Storytelling', largely concerned to propose that there is little evidence for extended narrative structures, including the epic, in pre-literate societies, posits in passing that the late arrival of the novel proper in both Europe and China (roughly in the sixteenth century) has to do with the late emergence of a 'positive' category of fiction which understands it in each case as something other than mere untruth. Henry Zhao's more detailed exploration of the ways in which 'the very idea of fictionality baffled Chinese thinking' analyses a

REVIEW

cultural configuration in which fictional writing is perceived as a supplement to a dominant and legitimate historiography, and must justify itself on those grounds. In their essay, Michal Ginsburg and Lorri Nandrea draw on Hegel's notion of the 'prose of the world' in his *Aesthetics: Lectures on Fine Art* (1835)—'a world of finitude and mutability, of entanglement in the relative, of the pressure of necessity from which the individual is in no position to withdraw'—to argue that the novel, built on an ethos of the relative and the contingent, establishes its authority by an appeal not to the person of the performer (as do the poetic genres that precede it) but—quite paradoxically, of course—to referential truth. And Francesco Orlando has a long and interesting discussion of the forms and the conditions of possibility of the supernatural in literature, defining that genre in terms of its refusal to conform to the novel's conventions of plausibility.

But the most informative essay in this cluster is 'The Rise of Fictionality', Catherine Gallagher's superb genealogy of the category of the fictional in eighteenth-century Europe. What she isolates for attention is the novel's odd ambivalence towards fictionality, 'at once inventing it as an ontological ground and placing severe constraints upon it'. Her essay traces a process in which the concept of fiction is slowly transformed in the course of the eighteenth century from an older meaning of 'deceit' to a semantic force which is something like 'the imaginary', a category which is nevertheless close to the real and therefore not merely fantasy. In this process, novelistic verisimilitude ceases to be a defensive (and always contestable) invocation of the truth of fact and becomes a more sophisticated suspension of disbelief, an epistemological category combining make-believe with the plausibility of the lifelike. It is this 'widespread acceptance of verisimilitude as a form of truth, rather than a form of lying, [that] founded the novel as a genre . . . It also created the category of fiction'. From this consolidation of the category of fiction comes, eventually, a less anguished relation to those genres that claim a directly referential access to the real. Fiction as the epistemological ground of the novel takes on its own legitimacy as 'a special way of shaping knowledge through the fabrication of particulars'. At the same time, the always-provisional verisimilitude of fiction, its poised balancing of the *true* and the *seeming*, comes to mesh with some of the deepest impulses of modernity, which Gallagher describes as:

> fiction-friendly because it encourages disbelief, speculation, and credit. The early novel's thematic emphasis on gullibility, innocence deceived, rash promises extracted, and impetuous emotional and financial investments of all kinds point to the habit of mind it discourages: faith.

In this respect the novel becomes a kind of training ground in the analysis of motives and in treating various types of stories (both the true and the made-up) as 'a kind of suppositional speculation'. More generally, she argues, 'almost all of the developments we associate with modernity—from greater religious toleration to scientific discovery—required the kind of cognitive provisionality one practises in reading fiction, a competence in investing contingent and temporary credit'.

This, I think, gets at what is epistemologically innovative about the novel form, and thus at some of the reasons for its social centrality over the last two to three centuries. Unlike many other, more metaphorical attempts to map the relation between literary and social forms, it specifies the pathways from the one to the other. It also has useful implications for thinking about fictional character, which Gallagher describes in terms of structures of identification made possible precisely by the make-believe nature of the novel's quasi-persons: it is the very unreality of literary characters, or rather the 'mutual implication of their unreal knowability and their apparent depth, the link between their real nonexistence and the reader's experience of them as deeply and impossibly familiar', that gives them their 'peculiar affective force'.

Historical analysis here shifts imperceptibly into an account of the formal categories that organize narrative—an analysis that transcends the period of European history with which Gallagher is concerned, but which can nevertheless be specified historically. Let me turn, then, to that more 'formalist' line of analysis which I have loosely associated with the work of Bakhtin and which I think is relatively under-represented in this collection. In one sense, of course, almost all of the essays in these two volumes are concerned with formal structures, especially those of genre; too many of them, however, are descriptive rather than analytic. Too few explore formal categories in the kind of depth that is required, and key categories—irony and time, to take two that Lukács isolates as core features of the genre—are largely absent, although Fredric Jameson has a characteristically authoritative account of the workings of providential time from its theological origins through its role in the *Bildungsroman* to its reincarnations in nineteenth-century realism and contemporary film. Alex Woloch's essay on minor characters in the novel goes in interesting ways to the question of the novelistic representation of persons but is, unfortunately, no more than a summary of his book published in 2003 on the structural role of minor characters, *The One vs the Many*. Andreas Gailus's essay on the German novella, 'Form and Chance', is imaginative and insightful in its reading of the structure of that unusually well-defined genre. The essay that most powerfully embodies this strand of analysis, however, is Mieke Bal's 'Over-writing as Un-writing: Descriptions, World-Making and Novelistic Time'—a careful unpicking of the functions of description in the novel. We tend to think of description as a kind of stasis, the frozen time of a quasi-pictorial representation; but in a series of close readings of narrative passages Bal isolates and explores the peculiar temporality of description, or rather the way it activates the 'fundamental heterogeneity' of time, in order then to argue for its centrality (rather than, as is usually assumed, its marginality) to narrative, as well as the particular ways in which it both interrupts and drives forward storytelling in the novel.

This is an immensely rich collection, and I have barely touched on some of the most interesting work, much of which is contained in the sections that Moretti calls 'Readings' (brief analyses of particular texts) and 'Critical Apparatus'. The latter comprises, in Volume One, a section on 'The Semantic Field of Narrative', which explores a set of overlapping terms for structures and genres of storytelling: the Hebrew *midrash*, the Greek and Latin terms *mythos* and *fabula*, *monogatari*, *xiaoshuo* (literally 'small-talk'), the Arabic *qissa*, romance (with its variant forms in the Romance languages), and the Old-Russian *povest*. The other component of the Critical Apparatus is a series of statistical profiles of the market for novels in Europe, the US, Japan, India, Latin America and Africa. The Readings are more diverse and of unequal value: in Volume One a section called 'Traditions in Contact' looking at six novels from Lebanon, Japan, Turkey, Korea, South Africa and Iran, and another on novels from the Americas; and in Volume Two, a section on generic 'prototypes': the *Aethiopika* of Heliodorus, the tenth-century *Maqamat*, *Lazarillo de Tormes*, Madeleine de Scudéry's *Le Grand Cyrus*, Montesquieu's *Persian Letters*, Scott's *Waverley*, Sue's *Mysteries of Paris*, and Wells's *War of the Worlds*; a section on political novels; a section on 'The Sacrifice of the Heroine'; another on 'The New Metropolis' (novels thematizing and celebrating Shanghai, Buenos Aires, Lagos, Cairo, Havana, Bombay, and Istanbul); and a final section on experimental novels, from Rilke's *Malte Laurids Brigge* to Pynchon's *Gravity's Rainbow*.

Almost all of this is, at the least, informative, and much of the information has to do with traditions that are likely to be unfamiliar to many readers; the very fact of their unfamiliarity tells us something about the way the canon of the novel has been constructed. More generally, the collection's emphasis on the 'polygenesis' of the novel and on the wide range of archaic and cognate forms with which it shares the field of narrative is immensely valuable. What I take from it is a sense not so much of the value of comparative study (something for which several contributors argue) as of the value of differential analysis within a comparative framework. By entitling this collection 'The Novel' Moretti seems to suggest the unity and coherence of the form; but the force of the diversity of topics and forms it embraces is to underline the sheer heterogeneity of the genres of the novel.

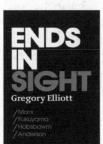
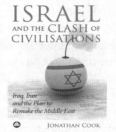

John Lewis Gaddis, *The Cold War*
Penguin: London 2007, £8.99, paperback
333 pp, 978 0 14 102532 2

John Lewis Gaddis, *Surprise, Security and the American Experience*
Harvard University Press: Cambridge, MA and London 2005,
£8.95, paperback
150 pp, 978 0 674 018365

ANDERS STEPHANSON

SIMPLICISSIMUS

John Lewis Gaddis has been one of the most ideological figures within the subfield of US 'diplomatic history'. All historians, of course, operate in and through ideology; Gaddis, however, has been unusual in foregrounding the ideological nature of his works. Though the message to be conveyed has not always been the same, he has been constant in his defence of US interests, and has consistently mirrored—albeit with slight lags—the prevailing attitudes of the powers that be. A realist in the 1970s and neo-Reaganite from the late 1980s onwards, Gaddis was somewhat disgruntled in the Clinton era, but has found the second Bush altogether more congenial. Gaddis's method, too, has endured across his extensive œuvre: always disdainful of any excessive fascination with the archives, he has preferred to pick out some theme or idea and drive it through with relentless single-mindedness and clarity, subordinating every aspect of the proceedings to his ideological aim. His characterization of Ronald Reagan in his most recent book, *The Cold War*, applies equally to himself: 'His strength lay in his ability to see beyond complexity to simplicity'.

For Gaddis, the right kind of simplicity is not truth simplified, but truth itself. Contradiction, nuance and uncertainty tend to disappear from his work. This does not necessarily make it uninteresting: it takes a certain intelligence, confidence and ruthlessness to write this kind of history.

REVIEW

Gaddis published his dissertation on *The United States and the Origins of the Cold War* in 1972, and has been writing prolifically about the same topic since then, remaining essentially within its political framework. At the beginning of his career, his project was to defuse the revisionist critique of America's responsibility for the early Cold War, nationalist orthodoxy having been largely shot to pieces by Vietnam. It was, if you will, a containment strategy against revisionism—seeking to preserve the 'truth' of orthodoxy while making some concessions to the other side. Bored by such historiographical controversies, however, Gaddis began to move away from his own discipline in the mid-1970s, turning instead to the field of international relations. The shift was hardly surprising: his governing interest has always been policymaking at its most elevated, and neo-realist theory provided him with a means of reaching his ideal Beltway audience. Initially, the change in approach proved fertile, resulting in some of his best works: *Strategies of Containment* (1982) and *The Long Peace* (1986) are both products of this moment, where the combination of Gaddis's neorealist idiom and his close attention to the protocols of empirical evidence put a damper on any indiscriminate US nationalism.

With the disappearance of the USSR, however, Gaddis became disenchanted with international relations theory, mainly because of its—and his—failure to grasp the changes taking place during the 1980s in the Soviet Union and international system; after all, in *The Long Peace*, Gaddis himself had celebrated the stability of the Cold War at the very moment when it was coming to an end. He now began to slide to the right, under the towering influence of Reagan, and to seek inspiration in whatever areas happened to serve his ideological concerns of the moment. Hence his intermittent interest in chaos theory, plate tectonics and, in *The Cold War*, theatrics and drama. This sounds a lot more intellectually adventurous than it really is, since Gaddis's approach is always eminently reductionist.

Outside the academic world, and certainly outside the US, Gaddis has come to be seen as the most distinguished representative of diplomatic history, although he has distanced himself from its scholarly proceedings for quite some time, and is probably no longer considered central to the field by his colleagues. In 1997, he returned to his original area of expertise with *We Now Know: Rethinking Cold War History* (the unconvincing message of which was that Stalin was not only a communist but a romantic). Since moving from Ohio to Yale the same year, however, Gaddis has focused predominantly on 'Grand Strategy'—which he has described, typically, as an intuitive skill, requiring 'a certain shallowness'; no accident, then, that he has found avid readers in the Bush White House. But Gaddis has stayed notably clear of direct links to party politics. Originally from rural Texas, he has retained his domestic roots in traditional New Deal Democracy. Guarding his role as an 'independent' academic with the detachment and objectivity of a truth-telling historian has not only allowed him tactical room for manoeuvre; it is also the ultimate condition of his power.

Gaddis's latest opus on the Cold War has sold vastly more than any comparable work, and been widely regarded—again, outside the profession—as the authoritative word on the subject. Announced in its subtitle as 'a new history', the book is, from a scholarly viewpoint, nothing of the kind. Gaddis, defiantly, says as much himself, stating that he wrote the book in response to pleas from his agent and students for a more 'accessible' account, covering 'more years in fewer pages'. What we get is a set of undergraduate lectures, pulpit wisdom for a sympathetic and credulous audience. The narrative focuses on 'visions', good and evil, and how individual actors, good and evil, put them across in material settings; though with the exception of some perceptive passages about the nuclear game, the material aspect gets rather perfunctory attention. The Cold War was caused, not surprisingly, by Stalin, a very evil man indeed. Though he did not really want war, either hot or cold, Stalin got the latter because, just like Hitler, he sought to dominate Europe, thus eventually generating the kind of Western response he deserved. While the West at the end of the Second World War believed in the compatibility of incompatible systems—coexistence, if you will—Stalin believed that incompatible systems were precisely that. The shared victory of 1945 concealed the fact that the two systems were already at war, 'ideologically and geopolitically'. While the West was characterized above all by Hope, Stalin coupled Hope with pervasive Fear, which was to overshadow the world for the next five years.

The 1950s and the start of the nuclear arms race on a grand scale, however, brought a paradoxical lightening of the horizon: Gaddis describes the first American and Soviet hydrogen bomb tests of 1952–53 as 'a small but significant sign of hope for the human race'. For the massively increased lethality of the hydrogen bomb heralded what was to be confirmed in the Cuban Missile Crisis in 1962, namely, that no one could afford to let the Cold War turn into a hot one. The eve of destruction, then, provided for control and predictability, the kind of managed conflict that would receive its apotheosis in the détente of the 1970s. Alas, it was a false Hope. It was false, of course, because it left in place that unnatural command system, based on Fear, in the unnaturally extended East. While, for instance, Western occupations of Japan and Germany had been based on genuine self-determination, democracy, spontaneity and pragmatism, the Eastern system was one of command, repression, rigidity and a dogmatic belief in Theory over Practicality.

Meanwhile, in the same period 'autonomous' agents began to emerge: on the one hand the decolonized and non-aligned regimes, on the other free-wheeling 'high-wire acrobats' within the two Cold War camps—

pre-eminently, Mao and De Gaulle. The Cultural Revolution and May 68, respectively, brought the latter two down to earth, in Mao's case meaning the geopolitical opening to the United States. Little did the practitioners of realist statecraft realize that the return of Morality was just around the corner, heralded symbolically by Nixon's exit: the Constitution proved 'an adversary more powerful than either the Soviet Union or the international communist movement'. Thus, by the mid-1970s, a critical sense developed that there was indeed still a universal standard of justice. And what could be more obviously unjust than the geopolitical stability game known as détente? Nixon, after all, had ended up defending, in the name of détente, the internal stability of the Soviet Union: sordid Watergate was commensurate with the sordid compromises of the Cold War. As the decade wore on, the United States recovered its moral and political bearings, the Soviet Union declined economically and, partly led astray by Fidel, went berserk in the Third World; the stage was ready for the triumphant return of everlasting notions of Morality and Evil.

'Stage' is indeed the proper word, for the world-historical agents who effected this monumental shift were all 'actors' in the dramatic sense as well. The prophet here was Pope John Paul II, the erstwhile Polish actor who called the Soviet bluff in Eastern Europe and revealed the depth of its legitimacy crisis. He, along with other visionaries such as Margaret Thatcher, Lech Wałęsa, Deng Xiaoping, and, above all, Ronald Reagan, radically questioned the verities of the Cold War system.

Reagan's decisive contribution was to see that the Cold War was merely a convention, immorally institutionalized in the game of nuclear balancing, and, equally immorally, legitimating the historical perversity known as the Soviet Union. Thus he attacked the whole idea of détente—that 'the Soviet Union had earned geopolitical, economic, and moral legitimacy as an equal to the United States'. Further, Reagan had grasped 'that the Soviet Union, its empire, its ideology—and therefore the Cold War itself—was a sandpile ready to slide.' If pushed, the whole edifice would collapse. We know the end: 'The Triumph of Hope', in the title of Gaddis's climactic chapter. Gorbachev deserves credit for not unleashing violence; but 'the most deserving recipient ever of the Nobel Peace Prize' of course lacked a 'vision' proper. The Hope he offered, a kind of humanized socialism and the preservation of the Soviet Union, had no foundation and deservedly perished.

What can be said of this fantasy? There are passages of eloquence and analytical depth, especially on nuclear weapons, where Gaddis succinctly sets out the strategic implications for both sides of the unprecedented destructive power they now possessed. But on the whole, Gaddis presents a morality play which verges on a fairy tale. It would be easy to target the astonishingly idealized vision of pristine US virtue, from the initial proposition that the

United States in 1945 was the 'freest place' on earth to pontifications about the West's flexibility, practicality, ideological openness and so forth. There is little sense in arguing against this idyll, faith-based as it largely is. When we are told, however, that the revolutions in Eastern Europe crushed the idea 'that governments could base their legitimacy on an ideology that claimed to know the direction of history', it is hard not to see inadvertent irony: if any regime is built on the idea that it knows the direction of history, it is that of the US, as condensation of universal history and end of history in freedom. Gaddis, in fact, is unknowingly reiterating the basic theme of NSC 68, one of the foundational early Cold War documents: whereas freedom is natural and stands on its own, totalitarianism—like all forms of slavery—is entirely parasitic and cannot exist except as an attack on freedom, its antithesis. The effect of this vision is well known: there can be no legitimacy for the enemies of freedom, for how could opposition to the natural and universal standards of justice be acceptable? This, in my view, is what made the Cold War a Cold War: the US refusal after 1947 to accord the Soviet Union any geopolitical legitimacy, even as an enemy. Grounded in the putative historical lessons of the 1930s and the ensuing World War, it was this that enabled the Truman Administration to effect the massive, permanent peace-time entry of the United States into world politics.

Gaddis's scheme ensures there are no doubts about the justness of the Cold War's outcome: 'the world, I am quite sure, is a better place for that conflict having been fought in the way that it was and won by the side that won it.' This established, the only thing that remains to be determined is how well the Empire of Liberty executed its historically appointed task, and to hand out appropriate marks to the various actors in the story. What, for Gaddis, almost led the Empire astray was the nuclear balance of terror and certain counter-productive excesses, geopolitical and ethical, in the local fight against communism—the one by implying recognition of its opponent as an equal, the other by allowing freedom to become somewhat contaminated. While Gaddis understands entirely the mechanisms that impelled the US in the 1960s to come to terms, relatively speaking, with the Soviet Union, what animates his story is 'the return of equity'—the stunning reversal of the 1980s, as a reawakened US, under the leadership of the Great Communicator, vigorously challenged an increasingly decrepit Evil Empire.

In empirical terms, the storyline demands the least violence to historical nuance in its middle parts, the moments of putative excess and recognition. The early and late periods, conversely, require quite a great deal of it. Take, initially, Gaddis's account of 'origins'. It is simply not true that the Western powers and the Soviet Union were ideologically and geopolitically at war in 1945. Nor, arguably, did Stalin pursue a policy, either during the War or immediately afterwards, that went beyond the scope of traditional (tsarist) geopolitics; nor did he assume that the basic great-power constellation of the War could not continue. Stalin was a hyper-realist. His outlook, and that of the Communist movement, was that of anti-fascist alliance politics, deemed (perhaps wrongly) to be in the long-term interests of his regime and the auxiliary movement he so often found a nuisance. Hence the extraordinarily conservative policy of the Communist Parties in France and Italy, the only ones with any real power in Western Europe, as they helped substantially to reconstruct capitalism in their respective countries until they were thrown out of the coalition governments in 1947. Hence too Stalin's incredulity at the revolutionary examples of Tito's Yugoslavia and Mao's China, and his subsequent suspicion, not unwarranted from his vantage point, of their essentially independent nature.

Gaddis's pivotal moment of reversal is even more spurious. The notion that the Reagan Administration could be featured within some general return to morality and universal standards of justice is nothing short of darkly amusing: it is hard to find another postwar US administration that so flagrantly and massively broke all rules of international conduct. Iran-Contra? Not mentioned. Arming pathological killers in El Salvador? Illegal mining of Nicaraguan harbours? Not mentioned. Support for South African apartheid and Saddam Hussein? Not mentioned. Almost in passing, Gaddis notes that Reagan's nuclear musings and moves came recklessly close to causing real war.

There remains the insurmountable problem called the People's Republic of China. Where does it fit in Gaddis's scheme? How could the United States virtually ally itself with the most radical of Communist regimes, which was not even diplomatically recognized, against a far more conservative one, officially committed to the idea of peaceful coexistence? On these issues, Gaddis offers nothing but cursory remarks, murmuring vaguely that the consensus on China is still unclear—as though any such consensual clarity would have mattered to him. This reticence stems from a certain ambiguity on the foundational question of whether the Cold War was a systemic conflict. If a utopian communist such as Mao could decide, on 'realistic' grounds, to ally with the US, and if the US could ally with him in the name of triangulation, what systemic dimension could there possibly be?

Gaddis does not confront this problem, because his overwhelming desire is not to explain the nature of the Cold War as such, but to recount the triumph of democratic capitalism over totalitarian communism. The end is thus inscribed in the beginning, which is why he has to insist that the whole period or system is essentially the same throughout. The story of timeless goodness requires that 1989–91 must be about 1945–47. That there was a US reversal and that the Soviet Union disappeared is not, of course, in doubt. However, the Soviet Union did not collapse, it was destroyed. Historical accident also played a significant role: Chernobyl arguably had a greater impact on internal divergences at the Soviet top than Reagan's posturings. But these are complex historical problems that dreary clichés about decline, decrepitude and moral challenges do little to illuminate.

Historians may object to Gaddis's simplifications, but they go a long way among undergraduates, political scientists and presidents. George W. Bush would likely find the political tenor and plain talking of *The Cold War* much to his taste. In any event, in 2004 the President—without prompting—read Gaddis's *Surprise, Security, and the American Experience,* a very short book which purports to show that Bush's policy of pre-emption is thoroughly and safely within the historical traditions of US foreign policy. In Gaddis's view the War on Terror, invasion of Afghanistan and Operation Iraqi Freedom represent only an adaptation, if necessarily a radical one, of an underlying matrix dating back as far as 1814 when, after the British occupied and burnt down Washington, DC, John Quincy Adams articulated the three methods by which American security should be assured. Bush is in fact merely the last in a long line of US leaders who have engaged in 'pre-emption', 'unilateralism' and 'hegemony'. Behind this American trinity, however, lies an even more fundamental continuity in the country's way of being towards the world: when threatened, the United States tends not to contract its security sphere but expand it aggressively—most saliently at moments when the homeland is subjected to direct, surprise hits (1814, 1941, 2001).

On this view, the Second World War and ensuing Cold War were aberrations. For Roosevelt, saddled after 1941 with difficult military exigencies, could not practice either pre-emption or unilateralism, and the necessities of the Cold War—alliances, nuclear weapons—also dictated reliance on 'hegemony' alone. Reagan defeated the Evil Empire, of course, but in the 1990s, just when objective conditions were ripe for the final eradication of tyranny, there was a failure of American nerve and vision. Clinton and his ilk, devoid of a Grand Strategy or any sense of History, imagined that capitalist globalization would by itself take care of matters. The depth of this illusion was revealed by the incomprehensibly evil deeds of September 11, which set the stage for George W. Bush's metamorphosis into 'the first great grand strategist of the 21st century'—'one of the most surprising transformations of an underrated national leader since Prince Hal became Henry V'.

The Bush Doctrine of 2002 was the properly deterritorialized response to a new kind of deterritorialized threat: intervening anywhere and everywhere, should the occasion so require. In today's world, 'respecting sovereignty is no longer sufficient because that implies a game in which the players understand and respect the rules. In this new game there are no rules.' A strategy of pre-emption, unilateralism and hegemony is what is called for, this time on a global scale. Bush's method for defusing the threat of terrorism, meanwhile, is 'breathtakingly simple: it is to spread democracy everywhere'. For terrorism has nothing to do with the US or Israel, and everything to do with the frustrations of living in tyrannical or authoritarian Islamic socie- ties. Gaddis is much more interested in altering society than in terrorism as such—'regime change', in the terminology of choice. The dominant idea is to initiate the democratic transformation of the Middle East, bringing it into the 'modern world', and thus finally to realize the Wilsonian vision of a world made safe for democracy.

Gaddis portrays the early phases of this strategy's implementation in the most enthusiastic terms:

> The Bush Administration got a taste of Agincourt with its victory over the Taliban at the end of 2001, to which the Afghans responded by gleefully shav- ing their beards, shedding their burkas, and cheering the infidels—even to the point of lending them horses from which they laser-marked bomb targets.

After this stunning success, the US could confidently march onward to Iraq, where a range of world-historical missions could be accomplished. Here is Gaddis ventriloquizing Bush:

> We could complete the task that the Gulf War left unfinished. We could destroy whatever weapons of mass destruction Saddam might have accumu- lated since. We could end whatever support he was providing for terrorists beyond Iraq's borders, notably those who acted against Israel. We could liber- ate the Iraqi people. We could ensure an ample supply of inexpensive oil. We could set in motion a process that could undermine and ultimately remove reactionary regimes elsewhere in the Middle East, thereby eliminating the principal breeding ground for terrorism.

This was of course the view of the then dominant neo-cons—but one they shared, it should be recalled, with a number of liberal interventionists. It no doubt explains the White House's enthusiasm for the book; Gaddis was even invited to help the President work out some of the passages on pre-emption in his inaugural speech of January 2005. By that time, of course, as the difficulties in Mesopotamia were becoming obvious, Gaddis was having second thoughts about the invasion; in the latter stages of *Surprise*, he gives greater symbolic salience to the figure of Bismarck, who knew not only when to shock and awe but also, prudently, when to stop. Nonetheless, the US remains the home of Liberty: 'we are, if not the last hope of earth, then certainly in the eyes of most of its inhabitants still the best'.

Five years after the shock and awe it is not obvious that anyone remem- bers the idea of a Bush Doctrine. But despite its ephemerality, Gaddis is right, for the wrong reasons, to have insisted that it was a real shift. At no time in the history of the United States has anyone ever declared the supreme right to do whatever one chooses wherever one chooses—in effect, global sovereignty. One should not trivialize this move, which took the leeway already granted by Clinton's 'humanitarian interventionism' a decisive step farther. Otherwise, however, the book is largely yet another ideological exercise, in which Gaddis superimposes the ruling concerns of the present onto the past. Normalizing and naturalizing Bush as an innovative traditionalist is vintage Gaddis: rather than sanitizing the president by dressing him up in nicer imagery, he provides Bush with historical pedigree, making him a latter-day John Quincy Adams. As in *Cold War*, the end is present in the beginning. The procedure is circular: the Bush Doctrine is projected backwards and found to be the traditional 'Truth of America', which can then be traced forwards to its properly American end in the very same Bush Doctrine.

Gaddis's overall argument—that the US has a long history of pre-emption and unilateralism—might seem a fairly accurate depiction of US imperialism, if inverted; the good here being bad. Empirically, alas, the problem is that the whole is false. While the United States has certainly engaged liberally in pre-emption, this has not always or even chiefly been part of any 'Grand Strategy', or due to notions of security or insecurity. The territorial expansion of the 19th century likewise had little to do with Grand Strategy, but was rather heavily imbricated in, and indeed largely preconditioned by, relatively autonomous economic interests and processes. The United States, not to put too fine a point on it, was about more and better capitalism. More particularly, to the extent that there was a 'security surprise' that enlarged US conceptions of its interests in the 19th century, it was not the burning of the tiny provincial city of Washington by Admiral Cockburn in 1814, but the Black Jacobin revolution in Haiti, which not only scared the wits out of the slave-owning liberal Thomas Jefferson, but, ironically was also what ultimately allowed him to buy the Louisiana Territory from Napoleon, and so double the size of the country.

In any case, the occupation of Washington can scarcely have come as a surprise to the Americans since they themselves had declared war two years earlier, and had occupied York, capital of British Upper Canada, in 1813. The next huge addition of land, acquired after the aggression against Mexico of 1846–48, was similarly not the product of surprise but the combined result of frontier penetration, profitable cotton slavery and the promise of acquiring excellent harbours on the West Coast. It had nothing to do with 'pre-emption' in the sense that we will find after 9/11. Gaddis also misrepresents the Monroe Doctrine, which Adams composed in 1823 not in response to the war with the British, but to the crumbling of the Spanish Empire in Latin America. Adams, a complex and contradictory figure, was certainly an expansionist, but was sharply and unequivocally against intervention beyond the immediate vicinity of the existing borders, and certainly against interventionism in the name of extending 'liberty'.

Moreover, pre-emption, unilateralism and hegemony cannot be said to form a specifically 'American' trinity as Gaddis contends. Indeed, there is arguably no trinity at all: what makes the former two effective is, in the end, hegemony. Without this normative ingredient, pre-emption and unilateralism would become simple tools of classical statecraft, or, put differently, the military house rules of the state of Israel. This, not the redoubtable John Quincy Adams, seems the immediate model. The major shortcoming of Gaddis's account, however, is the projection of strategic coherence and lucidity. For explanations of US foreign policy are, on the contrary, for long periods marked by a strong arbitrariness, which is in turn an expression of several 'domestic' factors: the relative unimportance of foreign relations as such (with some spasmodic exceptions); the overwhelmingly domestic reproduction of the ruling classes; and a federalism which, paradoxically, at times affords an extraordinary licence to the monarchical presidency, not least because of his very real prerogatives as commander-in-chief. Within a certain ideological range, the White House has a remarkable latitude, which means that the character of its tenant can often matter more systemically to the outside than to the inside.

Gaddis's reputation as a historian, however, will not ultimately be determined either by his neo-Reaganite Cold War fable or his support for the Bush Doctrine, but by his forthcoming official biography of George Kennan. Like Adams a central figure in the annals of US foreign relations, Kennan is still more contradictory and difficult to handle, above all because he was capable of being so critical of both conventional policy and the United States as a society. His final act as a public intellectual—he died in 2005 at the imposing age of 101—had been to castigate the whole of Washington officialdom, including weak-kneed Democrats, for falling in with Bush's grossly wrongheaded invasion of Iraq. Such critical idiosyncrasies will not be processed so smoothly by the Gaddisian code machine, otherwise so effective in turning everything into a version of Gaddis himself.

Put Mind over Matter.

Get the TLS for less.

Half-price subscription offer to The Times Literary Supplement, the leading paper in the world for literary culture.

Great reasons to subscribe:

- Only £67 for a year's subscription - save 50% off the usual retail price*
- Exclusive online subscriber archive
- Delivered direct to your door every week - never miss an issue

To subscribe please call 01858 438 781, quoting code S026, or visit www.subscription.co.uk/tls/S026

* Offer available UK only. Rest of World (including ROI) prices start at £98 for 12 months.

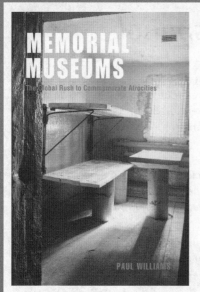